English for Job Interviews!

Veja como acessar o áudio p. 111

JOSÉ ROBERTO A. IGREJA
ROBERT C. YOUNG

English for Job Interviews!

UM GUIA COMPLETO PARA VOCÊ SE PREPARAR PARA
ENTREVISTAS DE EMPREGO EM INGLÊS

6ª Reimpressão

© 2008 José Roberto A. Igreja e Robert C. Young

Assistente editorial
Gabriela Canato

Preparação
José Muniz Jr. / Verba Editorial

Revisão
Flávia Yacubian

Capa e projeto gráfico
Paula Astiz

Editoração eletrônica
Lydia Megumi / Paula Astiz Design

Áudio
Locutores: Cory Willis, Richard Rafterman, Sarah Johnson
Produtora: JM Produção de áudio

Dados Internacionais de Catalogação na Publicação (CIP)
(Câmara Brasileira do Livro, SP, Brasil)

Igreja, José Roberto A.
  English for job interviews: um guia completo para você se preparar para entrevistas de emprego em inglês / José Roberto A. Igreja, Robert C. Young. - Barueri, SP : DISAL, 2008.

  Inclui áudio.
  ISBN 978-85-89533-93-5

  1. Entrevistas (Seleção de pessoal) 2. Entrevistas de emprego 3. Inglês - Estudo e ensino I. Young, Robert C.. II. Título.

08-00794 CDD-428

Índices para catálogo sistemático:
1. Entrevistas de emprego : Uso do inglês : Lingüística aplicada 428
2. Inglês : Uso em entrevistas de emprego : Lingüística aplicada 428

Todos os direitos reservados em nome de: Bantim, Canato e Guazzelli Editora Ltda.

Al. Mamoré 911, sala 107, Alphaville
06454-040, Barueri, SP
Tel./Fax: (11) 4195-2811

Visite nosso site: www.disaleditora.com.br

Vendas:
Televendas: (11) 3226-3111
Fax gratuito: 0800 7707 105/106
E-mail para pedidos: comercialdisal@disal.com.br

Nenhuma parte desta publicação pode ser reproduzida, arquivada nem transmitida de nenhuma forma ou meio sem permissão expressa e escrita da Editora.

SUMÁRIO

APRESENTAÇÃO	**7**

1. SAMPLE JOB INTERVIEWS AND VOCABULARY & EXPRESSIONS   9
Entrevistas-modelo de emprego e vocabulário & expressões

1.	Career in sales – Carreira em vendas	**9**
2.	Career in finance – Carreira em finanças	**11**
3.	Management interview – Entrevista para cargos gerenciais	**12**
4.	Changing job fields – Mudando de área de trabalho	**14**
5.	General job interview – Entrevista genérica de emprego	**15**
6.	Behavioral job interview – Entrevista comportamental de emprego	**16**
7.	Career in teaching – Carreira em ensino	**18**
8.	Informational job interview – Entrevista informativa	**19**
9.	Secretary job interview – Entrevista para secretárias	**20**
10.	Career in manufacturing – Carreira na indústria manufatureira	**21**
11.	An inappropriate interview – Uma entrevista inconveniente	**23**
12.	Career in information technology – Carreira em tecnologia da informação	**24**

2. KEY JOB INTERVIEW QUESTIONS   27
Perguntas-chave de entrevista de emprego

3. SAMPLE ANSWERS TO KEY JOB INTERVIEW QUESTIONS   35
Respostas-modelo às perguntas-chave de entrevista de emprego

4. INTERVIEWEE'S QUESTIONS   47
Perguntas do entrevistado

5. PRACTICE SETS   51
Exercícios práticos

6. PORTUGUESE-ENGLISH GLOSSARY   63
Glossário Português-Inglês

7. KEY TO PRACTICE SETS   103
Respostas aos exercícios práticos

8. AUDIO GUIDE - TRACK AND PAGE   107
Guia do Áudio – Faixa e página

SOBRE OS AUTORES	**109**
COMO ACESSAR O ÁUDIO	**111**

APRESENTAÇÃO

É com muito prazer e satisfação que apresentamos **English for Job Interviews!**, um livro planejado para ajudar você a se preparar para entrevistas de emprego em inglês, algo cada vez mais comum no mundo corporativo brasileiro.

Ser entrevistado em inglês para um cargo ou função é uma situação muitas vezes descrita como tensa, mesmo por pessoas que se consideram razoavelmente fluentes no idioma. Afinal, a mudança do referencial lingüístico faz com que perguntas simples se tornem armadilhas para o entrevistado. Foi pensando nisso que desenvolvemos este material, que aborda a linguagem específica desse contexto. Este livro irá ajudá-lo a se sentir mais à vontade, ganhar autoconfiança e melhorar seu desempenho nas entrevistas de emprego em inglês.

O conteúdo do livro e do áudio de **English for Job Interviews!** irá ajudá-lo a:

» Conhecer, revisar e consolidar o vocabulário e as expressões em inglês empregadas em entrevistas de emprego, por meio do material apresentado nas quatro seções do livro. (Veja abaixo o item "As seções do livro")

» Praticar e preparar-se para a compreensão auditiva de perguntas comuns em entrevistas de emprego em inglês, com o uso do áudio, evitando surpresas.

» Familiarizar-se com roteiros e variações de contexto das entrevistas, a partir da leitura dos doze modelos apresentados. Você poderá também praticar a compreensão auditiva das doze entrevistas com o áudio.

» Tornar a comunicação durante entrevistas mais clara e objetiva.

AS SEÇÕES DO LIVRO

Sample job interviews (Entrevistas-modelo de emprego)

Essa seção traz 12 modelos de entrevistas de emprego, com variedade de temas e situações. Permite uma visão abrangente, tanto do vocabulário e das expressões, quanto dos assuntos abordados. Ao final de cada entrevista, você conta com o item **Vocabulary & Expressions**, com a análise de vocabulário e expressões. Uma ótima forma de explorar essa seção é o uso do áudio que acompanha o livro. Ele permite a você não apenas treinar a compreensão das entrevistas, mas também reciclar palavras e expressões e se familiarizar com a pronúncia.

Key job interview questions (Perguntas-chave de entrevista de emprego)

Essa seção apresenta as perguntas mais comuns e relevantes em entrevistas de emprego. Ao planejar sua resposta, você poderá sempre contar com o **Portuguese-English Glossary**, pesquisando o vocabulário e as expressões necessários para construir o que deseja responder. Tomamos o cuidado de apresentar as diversas maneiras de se perguntar a mesma coisa. Também agrupamos as perguntas afins, para facilitar a procura. Ao se preparar para uma entrevista em inglês, você poderá praticar ouvindo as perguntas-chave no áudio e fazendo uma pausa a cada pergunta, para responder em inglês.

Sample answers to key job interview questions
(Respostas-modelo às perguntas-chave de entrevista de emprego)
Essa seção apresenta modelos de resposta para as perguntas mais comuns e relevantes em entrevistas de emprego. É importante enfatizar que os modelos de resposta apresentados são apenas exemplos e sugestões a partir dos quais você poderá moldar suas próprias respostas. O objetivo principal é preparar você para as perguntas-chave, de tal modo que você possa pensar previamente no que deseja responder e planejar as suas respostas com o auxílio do **Portuguese-English Glossary**.

Interviewee's questions (Perguntas do entrevistado)
Ao longo de uma entrevista, haverá momentos em que você também vai querer fazer perguntas, e isso acontece como resultado natural da interação na conversa. Essa seção apresenta um roteiro com perguntas-chave, que o entrevistado pode oportunamente fazer ao entrevistador. O principal objetivo é que você visualize com clareza e exatidão como formular perguntas adequadamente, do ponto de vista gramatical e lexical do idioma.

Practice sets (Exercícios práticos)
Uma ótima maneira de revisar, consolidar e colocar em prática o vocabulário e as expressões usuais em entrevistas de emprego. Esta seção apresenta três tipos de exercício:
» **Fill in the blanks:** A partir de frases contextualizadas, mas incompletas, você deverá preencher as lacunas com palavras ou expressões do banco de vocabulário.
» **Matching:** Nesta atividade você deverá combinar a palavra ou expressão com sua respectiva definição.
» **Multiple choice:** Você deverá escolher a alternativa que melhor explica ou define a palavra ou expressão do enunciado.

O livro inclui as respostas de todos os exercícios, o que o torna um ótimo material para o estudo autodidático.

Portuguese-English Glossary (Glossário Português-Inglês)
Esta seção foi desenvolvida especificamente para a comunicação em entrevistas de emprego. Não apenas reúne o vocabulário e as expressões usuais desse tipo de situação, mas também apresenta exemplos contextualizados e traduzidos. O objetivo principal do glossário é servir como fonte de consulta, tirar suas dúvidas e ajudá-lo a preparar suas respostas às perguntas-chave sobre aviso prévio, hora extra, licença-maternidade, terceirização, fusão comercial, rotatividade de funcionários, turno de trabalho, concorrência e atendimento ao cliente. Inclui também traços de personalidade e habilidades específicas, elementos muito importantes em entrevistas de emprego.

1. SAMPLE JOB INTERVIEWS AND VOCABULARY & EXPRESSIONS

Entrevistas-modelo de emprego e vocabulário & expressões

ılı|ı TRACK 1 - CAREER IN SALES

Interviewer: So, did you find us easily?

Interviewee: It was no problem at all. You have a very beautiful view from your office.

Interviewer: Thank you. It is definitely one of the perks of the job. Would you like some coffee or water?

Interviewee: No, thank you.

Interviewer: Ok then. Well, looking at your résumé, it appears you have a lot of impressive experience in sales.

Interviewee: Thank you. Yes, I believe you can say it is my niche.

Interviewer: So, can you please tell me a little more about yourself.

Interviewee: I have over 12 years of sales and marketing experience. It's a job field that I love and I feel it brings the best out of me. I have a great ability to convince people and to build strong business relationships. As you can see from my résumé, I've been building up my experience by overcoming many challenges that have been presented to me.

Interviewer: What interest do you have in working here?

Interviewee: First, I believe your company has a great history and well respected product line. In the last 3 years, I've read that your earnings have grown by 33% and that your international market is booming. Secondly, I love challenges. I would love the opportunity to bring my sales and leadership experience to your team and feel that my expertise in market analysis could fit into this position.

Interviewer: Yes, we do anticipate many walls coming down in the international markets in the next year. Are you aware of our new line of medical scanners that we will introduce this year?

Interviewee: Yes I am. I have read that there is keen interest in Latin America and Eastern Europe for these.

Interviewer: We do think so ourselves, so we are keeping our fingers crossed. Are you comfortable working in an international environment?

Interviewee: Yes. Not only did I market and sale to Europe, but I speak Spanish and German and I am learning Portuguese right now.

Interviewer: I hear Portuguese is quite difficult.

Interviewee: It can be challenging, especially the verb conjugations. But since I already speak Spanish, it is not too difficult.

Interviewer: Can you tell me about a crisis you had to work through and what you did to solve the problem?

Interviewee: Two years ago at my previous company, we had an order for our most important client sent to the wrong address. It was our German client and they were quite angry to say the least. I was able to negotiate a new delivery date and coordinated a new shipment to be expedited immediately. After that I created a better after-sales service that produced a lot of positive feedback from our clients.

Interviewer: Sounds like it was a big headache. How do you handle stress? I am sure that you are quite aware that sales can have its ups and downs.

Interviewee: I prepare as much as I can before I go in for the sale. I think of every possible problem and what I would do to come up with a solution. If it comes to a boiling point, I take a quick walk outside if possible. When I am not at work, I ride my bicycle and swim. These activities keep me quite calm in and out of work.

Interviewer: Where would you like to see yourself in 5 years?

Interviewee: I would like to have a complete level of expertise in the sales and marketing arena which would enable me to head a complete division in a company such as yours. I want to perfect my leadership skills and to achieve all the goals I set for myself from the start of this job.

Interviewer: Sounds like some great goals to accomplish. The last question I would like to ask is what is your approach in sales?

Interviewee: I first like to build a relationship and connection to the potential client. I also listen very well to what they are saying. I think that is the most important skill. This is because you always need to know WHAT they want, not exactly what you want to sell them. I find that most of my clients notice and appreciate this approach.

Interviewer: Well, this all looks impressive. We are still going to interview a few more candidates, so if we are interested in a second interview, we will contact you this week.

Interviewee: I do appreciate your time and I do hope to hear from you.

VOCABULARY & EXPRESSIONS 1 - CAREER IN SALES

Perks: something that you get from your work in addition to the money you are paid, such as goods, meals, or a car. **»** Veja "benefícios" p. 68

Niche: a job, activity, position or place that is very suitable for someone. **»** Veja "nicho" p. 90

Bring the best out of someone: make someone behave in the best way that they can.

Building up my experience: increasing gradually my experience.

To overcome-overcame-overcome: to succeed in controlling or dealing with something.

Challenge: a situation or something that needs great mental or physical effort in order to be done successfully. **»** Veja "desafio" p. 75

Booming: growing rapidly. **»** Veja "aumentar; desenvolver-se rapidamente" p. 67
Expertise: special skill or knowledge in a particular subject. **»** Veja "competência" p. 70
To anticipate-anticipated-anticipated: to imagine or expect that something will happen.
We are keeping our fingers crossed: we are hoping that something will happen the way we want.
Come up with a solution: think of a solution.
Boiling point: a situation when things get really difficult and people can no longer deal calmly with a problem.
Arena: sphere of activity.
To enable-enabled-enabled: to make it possible for someone to do something.
To head/headed/headed: to lead or be in charge of.
To accomplish/accomplished/accomplished: to succeed in doing something; to achieve.
Approach: a way or method of doing something.

ılı｜ı TRACK 2 - CAREER IN FINANCE

Interviewer: Would you like some coffee or water before we begin?

Interviewee: No, thank you.

Interviewer: So, how long have you been out of university?

Interviewee: I just graduated in May.

Interviewer: I see that you studied economics at your university. What motivated you to major in this?

Interviewee: Ever since I was young, I've had an interest in all things financial. My father is in banking and used to show me what he did at his job. Being around numbers and money was so fascinating for me and I guess it is what drove me to major in economics.

Interviewer: In what ways did your degree help prepare you for a career in finance?

Interviewee: Most of the coursework I did was quite practical. We had many case studies that we had to solve. The course also offered a six month internship, which I did at the bank mentioned on my résumé. That was a wonderful opportunity because I got a great taste of day-to-day activities in finance.

Interviewer: Any specific things you learned on your internship that you feel you could bring to this position?

Interviewee: I was exposed to all areas of banking in my six months, so I feel that I have a decent foundation of the daily work that is needed at a bank. Specifically, I was able to sharpen my communication, analytical and problem solving skills. One of my duties was to analyze and chart the progress of one of our important client's investments. At times, I would have to contact them and communicate the findings I made. This really gave me an insight and strength in this area of the business.

Interviewer: Sounds like it was a very interesting experience. What are your strengths and weaknesses?

Interviewee: I feel that I have really developed strong analytical and organizational skills. At my internship, I created a new and improved system for analyzing and forecasting trends for local investors. I also organized a systematic way for it to be kept and communicated to the office. When I started the job, my phone skills were not that good. I was a little shy contacting people. But I worked with my manager every day to improve my verbal delivery and what to say when I called. After a few months, I lost my inhibitions and had no problem making calls to clients after that.

VOCABULARY & EXPRESSIONS 2 - CAREER IN FINANCE

To major in/majored in/majored in: to study something as your main subject at college.
Degree: title given to a college graduate.
Internship: a job that lasts for a short time, that a student does, in order to gain practical experience of a type of work. **»** Veja "estágio" p. 78
Foundation: base.
To sharpen/sharpened/sharpened: to improve.
Duties (pl.)/duty (sing.): something that you have to do because it is part of your job. **»** Veja "dever" p. 75
Findings: information that has been discovered.
Insight: a clear and sudden understanding of a complicated problem or situation.
Strengths (pl.)/strength (sing.): a positive quality that makes you more effective. **»** Veja "pontos fortes e pontos fracos" p. 94
Weaknesses (pl.)/weakness (sing.): a fault or lack of determination shown in someone's behavior. **»** Veja "pontos fortes e pontos fracos" p. 94
To forecast/forecast/forecast: to predict. .
Trends (pl.)/trend (sing.): prevailing tendency, direction or style.
Verbal delivery: the way in which someone speaks in public.

ılı|lı· TRACK 3 - MANAGEMENT INTERVIEW

Interviewer: So, I see from your résumé that you have over 7 years of managing experience? How would your colleagues describe your managing style?

Interviewee: I would have to say that they would describe me as open, fairly balanced and driven. I like to bring the best out of people.

Interviewer: Can you give me an example of how your drive improved the performance of your workers?

Interviewee: We had to improve our numbers by 12% in a 6 month period. It was going to be quite a challenge. First, I held a meeting to clearly define our goals for that period. I then gave each department a point system. If they achieved their targets every month, they would accumulate points. If they met all their goals, then we would have our 12% target at the 6 month point. The reward was a snazzy dinner paid by the company at one of the best restaurants in the city. I still had a backup plan to reward them even if they worked hard but didn't achieve the goal.

Interviewer: So you believe in rewarding even though they didn't make their target?

Interviewee: Absolutely. Goals are absolutely pertinent, but if they feel that their work only has merit if its countable by numbers alone, then I feel they will lose motivation.

Interviewer: Hmm, interesting insight. Have you ever had to fire an employee and if so, how did you approach the situation?

Interviewee: I have to say, that was the most difficult part of the job, but at times a necessary part. I had to let 4 people go in our department because of budget cuts. I met with each one personally. I made sure to point out all their successes and reiterate how much we appreciated their contribution to the company.

Interviewer: What factors are crucial within an organization and must be present for you to work most effectively?

Interviewee: For me, communication from the top is the most important. If I know exactly what is expected from me, it will be easier for me to perform my job. The organization must be positive too. Actually, these are some of the characteristics I find appealing at your company.

Interviewee: Thank you. We take pride in our quality of communication here.

VOCABULARY & EXPRESSIONS 3 - MANAGEMENT INTERVIEW

Driven (adj.): trying extremely hard to achieve what you want.
Bring the best out of people: make people behave in the best way that they can.
Drive: a planned, usually long-lasting effort to achieve something; determination.
Goal: an aim or purpose. » Veja "metas de vendas" p. 89
Target: a result or situation that you intend to achieve; aim; goal. » Veja "público-alvo" p. 95
Reward: something given in exchange for excellent work, etc. prize.
Snazzy (inf.): fashionable and attractive.
A backup plan: a second plan that you can use if the original one does not work or fails.
Insight: a clear and sudden understanding of a complicated problem or situation.
To approach/approached/approached: to deal with something.
I had to let 4 people go in our department: I had to fire 4 people in our department.

> **To reiterate/reiterated/reiterated**: to repeat a statement or opinion in order to make your meaning as clear as possible; to say something again.
> **Crucial**: vitally important; critical.
> **Appealing**: attractive; interesting.
> **Take pride in**: do something carefully and well.

𐄷ᏂᏂᏂᏆ TRACK 4 – CHANGING JOB FIELDS

Interviewer: Well, I guess the first question I have to ask could be the most obvious. Why are you changing from teaching to human resources?

Interviewee: Yes, it seems like a large jump. But I feel my 4 years as a teacher have actually given me many opportunities that are parallel with the HR field.

Interviewer: For example?

Interviewee: I was able to develop strong speaking and training skills as a teacher. I had the chance to develop and coordinate semester training for a group of teachers.

Interviewer: What do you feel separates you from other candidates with an HR background?

Interviewee: I have a strong ability to multitask. It is needed as a teacher. I have had to work under immense pressure, from students, principals and parents. So I feel I can handle many unique types of personalities. I had to be extremely organized to plan and train other teachers.

Interviewer: How about dealing with subjects such as compensation, pensions, and other specifics for HR. What can you bring into these areas?

Interviewee: There were actually a lot of administrative duties I had as a teacher and trainer. While it was the school administration that dealt with teacher compensation, I did have a lot of communication with the daily organizational and planning processes with the school administration. I would have to create and file reports for the teachers' and students' development.

Interviewer: Give an example of when you had a problem with a peer. How did you handle it?

Interviewee: I never really had any personal problems with any of the teachers. I had one situation where one of the teachers misinterpreted something I said. I found out from another teacher that this person was upset with me. To prevent this from turning into a blaze, I decided to talk to the teacher one-to-one. She seemed to appreciate the gesture and we actually became friends after that.

Interviewer: What personal characteristics do you feel you can bring this department?

Interviewee: I am very grounded and straightforward. I love a challenge and always set goals for myself, in and out of work. I feel I have a lot of integrity and am quite transparent. As I mentioned earlier, I have a lot of experience with various types of personality. So I think I could easily make the transition from academics to business.

VOCABULARY & EXPRESSIONS 4 - CHANGING JOB FIELDS

A large jump: a big change.
Background: previous experience or training.
To multitask: to do many things at the same time.
Specifics: exact details.
To handle/handled/handled: to deal with a situation or problem.
Peer: a person who has the same type of job as you.
Turning into a blaze: becoming a serious problem.
Talk to someone one-to-one: talk to someone personally.
Grounded: in control of your emotions.
Straightforward: frank; honest; direct.
Integrity: the quality of being honest and having strong moral principles; honesty.
Transparent: clear.

ılıllı· TRACK 5 - GENERAL JOB INTERVIEW

Interviewer: Says here you are from California. How long did you live there?

Interviewee: I lived there until I graduated from university. I moved here to Chicago to get my master's and I've lived here since.

Interviewer: I guess Chicago is quite different than California, especially with the weather, huh?

Interviewee: Yes, the weather has been the biggest adjustment I've had to make. But I really love Chicago. Very diverse and there is always something to do. Plus California is only a 3 hour plane flight from here. So it is not that bad.

Interviewer: Well, that's great you like it here. Maybe we should get started.
I first would like to ask you to describe yourself for me.

Interviewee: I've been working in this field for five years and I am constantly setting higher goals for myself. My past five years in this field have prepared me to take on challenges and opportunities like the one your company could present. I am a very committed person and very driven to meet my goals. I'm someone who loves to work in teams, but I can work autonomously if needed.

Interviewer: What specific goals have you established for your career so far?

Interviewee: When I first entered this field, I had an idea that I wanted to be in product development. But once I got the taste of managing, I fell in love with it. So I put my focus into being the best manager I could be. I took courses and established concrete goals for each year, 6 months and each month. My personal goal at this point is to move into a director position.

Interviewer: What is it that you like and dislike the most about your position now?

Interviewee: I love motivating people. I love establishing goals and pushing people to do their best to achieve them. Honestly, I am not a big fan of meetings. But I know that is part of the process. So instead of dreading them, I try to bring as many positive points to them as I can.

Interviewer: Interesting. I don't like meetings that much either (laughs). So, how would you define success?

Interviewee: For me, it is when you define what you want, set goals, and do everything in your power to achieve it. Maybe we can't always get exactly what we want. But I think if we learn from the process in attaining or not attaining our goals, that is what is important and my definition of success.

VOCABULARY & EXPRESSIONS 5 - GENERAL JOB INTERVIEW

Master's (inf.): a master's degree; a university degree that you can get by studying for one or two years after your first degree.
Diverse: varied or different.
Take on challenges and opportunities: accept challenges and opportunities.
Committed: willing to work very hard.
Driven (adj.): trying extremely hard to achieve what you want.
Autonomously: independently.
To dread/dreaded/dreaded: to feel extreme fear or reluctance; to feel anxious or worried about something that may happen.
To attain/attained/attained: to achieve, reach or accomplish.

ılı|ı TRACK 6 – BEHAVIORAL JOB INTERVIEW

Interviewer: Describe a situation in which you had to arrive at a compromise or guide others to a compromise.

Interviewee: Last year, my department and the Human Resources were at odds about a training program. I felt that the program that HR wanted was not in tune with the needs of my department and could have been too time consuming. We set up an appointment with HR to bring both points of views to the table. At first, I was very set in my ways to see through that we got our way. But then I decided to listen very well to the needs and benefits of the program that HR was pushing for. I then saw some of the merits. I did bend on some of the proposals and HR did for mine too. It became a win-win solution for both of us and both departments were able to meet their needs.

Interviewer: I'm glad that worked out for you. How have you handled conflict in the workplace?

Interviewee: Luckily, I've never had a confrontational situation with a co-worker. I have

Interviewer: had disagreements. My approach is always to listen to their needs and frustrations. The more you listen, the more you can "stand in their shoes". The more empathetic you can be. I feel it is a good way to demonstrate emotional intelligence.

Interviewer: Describe a time when you were faced with problems or stresses that tested your coping skills.

Interviewee: We had a situation two years ago where there was an order placed that we just couldn't fulfill in time. The stress level was tremendous on my department. The work had to be done and I was quite realistic that the order's demands couldn't be changed. I essentially set realistic goals for what I could achieve every day. I decided to stay grounded and focused on what needed to be done in the moment. I felt that also helped influence my co-workers and made the situation more tolerable.

Interviewer: Tell me about a time when you had to go above and beyond the call of duty in order to get a job done.

Interviewee: During the time that I just mentioned, I did go out of the way and set higher goals. That meant that I had to physically do more overtime on the weekends. But I also set more time managing goals which I believe created better results and definitely a more stable mind.

VOCABULARY & EXPRESSIONS 6 – BEHAVIORAL JOB INTERVIEW

Compromise: an agreement between two sides who have different opinions.
Were at odds about a training program: disagreed about a training program.
Not in tune with the needs of my department: not appropriate to the needs of my department.
Set in my ways: determined; not likely to change your opinion.
To see through that we got our way: to make sure we did what we wanted to.
A win-win solution / a win-win situation: one that will end well for everyone involved.
Meet their needs: have what they needed.
Stand in their shoes: put yourself in their position.
Empathetic: able to understand other people's feelings and problems.
Coping skills: ability to deal with a difficult problem or situation.
Go above and beyond the call of duty: do more than expected from you at work.
Grounded: realistic; pragmatic; in control of your emotions.
Overtime: time worked in addition to your usual job hours. » Veja "fazer hora extra" p. 80
Stable: mentally well-balanced.

ᴵᴵᴵᴵᴵᴵᴵ **TRACK 7 – CAREER IN TEACHING**

Interviewer: Thanks for coming today. Would you like some coffee or anything before we start?

Interviewee: Oh, no thank you. I'm fine. This is a very beautiful school you have. It has a lot of history, doesn't it?

Interviewer: Yes. We are quite proud of the reputation it has. It's a more traditional school, but we are quite modern too. Well, I guess we should start. Can you tell me a little more about your teaching experience?

Interviewee: I've been teaching for 12 years, primarily in high schools. During this time, I also worked part time at a junior high school teaching math. I have taught math, calculus, geometry and was the coach for the girls' volleyball team. I love what I do and have continued in my learning process by earning a master's degree in curriculum design.

Interviewer: Yes, I noticed you just received your master's. What are your future plans with this? Do you want to stay with teaching or move into administration?

Interviewee: I love teaching so much that it would be too difficult for me to give up. I would be interested in moving into educational consulting while teaching at the same time.

Interviewer: Great. So now let me ask you some specific questions about teaching. Can you tell me how you handle a disruptive classroom?

Interviewee: I have found through trial and error that yelling at them does not work. I did this more when I first started. But I normally have the students and myself create a "class constitution" on the first day. We make the "rules and laws of the class" to follow. I find this helps with having everyone participate. We create a point system where all the students start off with the same amount of points. If they break one of the rules, say speaking out of turn or inappropriate behavior, then that student would lose points based on the democratic rules.

Interviewer: Well, that sounds very creative. How about students who are too problematic to follow the rules or constitution?

Interviewee: If there are too many problems, I either confront them with humor or with a question. If that doesn't work, I have them meet me so I can talk more to them. I have a very strong ability to build good relationships with my students and parents. I think sometimes the disruptive students just need someone to listen to them.

VOCABULARY & EXPRESSIONS 7 - CAREER IN TEACHING

Primarily: mainly; mostly.
Coach: a person who is responsible for training a team.

Master's degree: a university degree that you can get by studying for one or two years after your first degree.
Curriculum design: planning of the subjects that are taught by a school or the things that are studied in a particular subject.
To handle/handled/handled: to deal with a situation or problem.
Disruptive: causing problems.
Through trial and error: testing many different ways of doing something in order to find the best.
Wisely: having or showing good judgment; prudently.
To yell/yelled/yelled: to shout or say something very loudly.
Speaking out of turn: speaking when you shouldn't; when it's not your turn to do so.

ıɪ|ı|ıı TRACK 8 – INFORMATIONAL JOB INTERVIEW

Employer: So, how long have you been living in the city?
Job seeker: Just for a couple of weeks.
Employer: Any leads so far?
Job seeker: Yes, I have about three so far. Not really sure how they are going to turn out, but I'm keeping my fingers crossed. Again, thank you for taking the time to see me today. Would it be okay for me to start my questions?
Employer: Sure.
Job seeker: First I would like to ask about the daily duties of your job. What kind of skills would I need to succeed in this field?
Employer: You have to have a lot of patience with people. It can get quite busy at times and you have to have a cool head. As for every day, I first come into the office and check the agenda, e-mails, and daily tasks. I have meetings with my staff to go over the daily goals. There is a lot of goal setting and number crunching. I then spend about two hours making calls to potential clients. Sometimes I have to meet potential clients and current clients outside the office. There can be a lot of fires to put out. That's what makes this a stressful job at times.
Job seeker: Okay. What kind of long-term career opportunities exist in this exact field?
Employer: My goal is to become a director in a couple of years. It takes about 7 years of earning your stripes to do so. You can also go into a different direction than a director. There are many different departments you can go into.
Job seeker: If it is not too inappropriate, I would like to ask you about salary. Is the compensation good for each job progression stage?
Employer: Yes. This field pays pretty well. Moving into management can pay quite well. But I will be honest; it is a lot of hours and hard work to get there.
Job seeker: How about the turnover? Is it high or do people stay at the same job for a while?

Employer: Honestly, it is a little high. You have to be able to handle stress. If you are balanced and organized with your time, you can do well at this job. But if stress gets to you too quickly, then it could be enough to make you want to quit.

VOCABULARY & EXPRESSIONS 8 - INFORMATIONAL INTERVIEW

Leads (pl.) / lead (sing.): any possible job opportunities given by a person or network; a piece of information that may help you.

Not really sure how they are going to turn out: I don't know exactly what is going to happen.

I'm keeping my fingers crossed: I'm hoping that things will happen the way I want.

Staff: a group of people who work for an organization, or for a manager in an organization.

Go over the daily goals: check carefully the daily objectives.

Goal setting: establishing objectives.

Number crunching: calculation in order to find an answer.

There can be a lot of fires to put out: there can be a lot of problems to solve.

Earning your stripes: to do something to show that you deserve a particular position and have the skills needed for it.

Turnover: the rate at which employees leave a company and are replaced. » Veja "rotatividade" p. 97

If stress gets to you too quickly: if stress affects you too quickly.

To quit/quit/quit: to leave a job without finishing it completely.

⑈⑈⑈ TRACK 9 - SECRETARY JOB INTERVIEW

Interviewer: So, I see here that you've been doing secretarial work for quite a while. What makes you want to stay in this profession?

Interviewee: I guess you can say that I enjoy the challenge of having many things to do at the same time. I am a very strong multitasker.

Interviewer: That is needed here, I can promise that. Can you tell me how you usually handle the stress of having so much thrown at you at the same time?

Interviewee: I believe being organized is the most important quality to have. I prioritize what needs to be done immediately vs. what can wait for a short amount of time. I keep my desk quite orderly and the same with my computer. It sounds simple, but it works.

Interviewer: Have you had to deal with a difficult manager in the past? If so, how did you handle it?

Interviewee: I have never had anyone who has been too difficult. But I did have a manager who could be quite moody. I would always be aware of his mood that day. I have a good sense of humor, so I would try to use that when it was needed.

Interviewer: What is your 5-year career plan?

Interviewee: My ambition is to be the secretary of the CEO one day. I am quite ambitious and would look forward to the highest level challenge like this.

Interviewer: What kind of salary are you looking for?

Interviewee: I understand that the market for someone with my skills is over $50,000. I would like something in that area.

Interviewer: How would you describe yourself in one sentence?

Interviewee: An ambitious and pragmatic ball of energy.

Interviewer: Hmm, looks like you have the best of both worlds. Can you tell me why you are leaving your present position?

Interviewee: I am ready for a new challenge. I have worked at my present job for 5 years and unfortunately there are not many positions for me to move into. From what I've read about your company, it appears that your new acquisition will give many more challenging opportunities within the company. I am quite confident that I could bring my energy and practical experience to benefit your company.

Interviewer: Possibly so. Thank you so much for coming in and we will let you know something next week.

VOCABULARY & EXPRESSIONS 9 - SECRETARY INTERVIEW

Multitasker: a person who does several things at the same time.

Handle the stress: deal with the stress.

Having so much thrown at you: having too much work given to you.

To prioritize/prioritized/prioritized: to arrange in order of importance so that you can deal with the most important things first.

Vs.: versus.

Moody: often sad, annoyed or unhappy or changing quickly from being happy to sad, for no clear reason.

CEO: chief executive officer; the person in charge of a group or organization. » Veja CEO p. 70

Pragmatic: dealing with problems in a sensible, practical way.

Acquisition: something obtained, esp. a company that has been bought or taken over. » Veja "aquisição" p. 65

ılıılı TRACK 10 - CAREER IN MANUFACTURING

Interviewer: You've been working in maintenance as a coordinator I see. What have you liked about the job?

Interviewee: I like the challenges the most. I work with the director to come up with ways to motivate and use the machines to their best capacity.

Interviewer: Have you had any big challenges at your last job that can display your leadership and communication skills?

Interviewee: My director created a new program for saving energy. For these changes to happen, I would have to train the staff to learn how to observe any energy loss the machines might have and how to be autonomous with their job.

Interviewer: Can you expand regarding your staff being autonomous please?

Interviewee: What my director and I decided to do was to train each machine operator to learn how to repair any problems that might happen to their machine. We also gave them new guidelines on how to better preserve energy. This was important because if the workers could repair their own machines, it would save a lot of time for me and my director.

Interviewer: Can you tell me how you handled an emergency situation, if you had one before. If not, how did you prepare for a possible crisis?

Interviewee: My director and I were given strict guidelines from our corporate headquarters on what do to. It was our job to train our staff. We would have emergency drills every two months. We also had monthly checks on the machines to make sure they were running properly.

Interviewer: Have you ever had to settle a conflict between two workers?

Interviewee: Never a strong conflict. But I have had disagreements and arguments that have happened. I believe in open communication and my door is always open. I would bring in one at a time to get their story and then both together after talking to them privately. I believe in listening and being empathetic. It always worked.

Interviewer: Manufacturing can be quite repetitive and stressful. Did you have any methods to help ease this with your staff?

Interviewee: Yes. I had a room that was called the "time-out room". This was where they could play cards, music or relax on a sofa during their break. They seemed to like this because it showed that we cared enough about them.

Interviewer: I see. The "time-out room" seems to be also a good place for employees complaining of Repetitive Strain Injury!

Interviewee: Definitely!

Interviewer: And what are your strengths in your opinion?

Interviewee: I am a strong communicator and motivator. I expect a lot from my workers, but I give a lot back as a leader. I am quite organized and have a systematic way of keeping track of overhead and maintenance problems.

VOCABULARY & EXPRESSIONS 10 - CAREER IN MANUFACTURING

Come up with ways: think of ways; find ways.

To display/displayed/displayed: to clearly show an attitude or quality by what you do or say.
Staff: a group of people who work for an organization, or for a manager in an organization.
Strict guidelines: severe policy or conduct.
Headquarters: the main building or offices used by an organization. » Veja "matriz; sede de empresa" p. 89
Emergency drill: an occasion when people practice what they should do in a dangerous situation; exercise; practice.
Running properly: working in an adequate or appropriate manner.
Settle a conflict: bring a conflict to an end.
Arguments (pl.)/argument (sing.): a situation in which two or more people disagree, often angrily; controversy; dispute.
Empathetic: able to understand other people's feelings and problems.
To ease/eased/eased: to relieve from distress; to lessen the tension of; to make easier.
Break: a period of time when you stop working in order to rest, eat, etc; an interruption; a short period of rest. » Veja "pausa; intervalo" p. 92
RSI: Repetitive Strain Injury. » Veja "LER: lesão por esforço repetitivo" p. 87
Strengths (pl.) / strength (sing.): a positive quality that makes you more effective. » Veja "pontos fortes e pontos fracos" p. 94
Keeping track of overhead: maintaining a record of general business expenses.

ı|ı|ıı TRACK 11 – AN INAPPROPRIATE INTERVIEW

Interviewer: Nice to meet you and please have a seat.

Interviewee: Thank you. Very nice layout you have in your office.

Interviewer: Well, thank you. We put a lot of thought into creating something more open and less suffocating. So if you could tell me what interested you in this position?

Interviewee: It seems like a challenging and rewarding position. I have 6 years in the field and I believe I could bring my specific experience in market research to the position. I am also excited with the last 3 years of growth in your company.

Interviewer: What challenges have you faced before in market research?

Interviewee: I worked in a smaller company that had a smaller market share. We had to be much more aggressive and more creative in our market research and presentation. I worked with my team to create a better market niche that was able to increase our share by 8%.

Interviewer: I notice on your resume that you are from Utah.

Interviewee: Yes, I was born there, but I've lived most of my life in California.

Interviewer: I understand. This job is quite demanding and will require you to do a good amount of traveling. Are you married or have any children? Just wondering if they would have problems with you moving around a lot.

Interviewee: I am sure they won't mind since I have traveled a lot with my previous job. I quite enjoy traveling.

Interviewer: Now how did you meet your wife exactly? I met mine here at work. Now don't tell anyone, but she was quite sexy and I just couldn't say no. So tell me your story.

Interviewee: Uhhh. I am sorry sir, but don't think this question is exactly relevant to the position that I am applying for. If you don't mind, I'd rather not answer. Can you tell me more about the position?

Interviewer: Oh come on! We are two guys. If you work here, you've gotta be careful because there are quite a few good looking ones!

Interviewee: I'm afraid that it seems like we are not a good match. I appreciate your time.

VOCABULARY & EXPRESSIONS 11 - AN INAPPROPRIATE INTERVIEW

Layout: the way in which something such as furniture is arranged.
Suffocating: uncomfortable because there is not enough fresh air.
Market share: the percentage of sales in a market that a company or product has.
Niche: a job, activity, position or place that is very suitable for someone. » Veja "nicho" p. 90
Demanding: expecting to have things exactly the way you want them.
We're not a good match: we don't go well together.

ılı|ı TRACK 12 - CAREER IN INFORMATION TECHNOLOGY

Interviewer: Come on in! Thank you so much for coming!

Interviewee: My pleasure! Thanks for having me! I must say right off the bat that I've only heard good things about your company.

Interviewer: Thank you! We do take pride in the way we do things here. I've read in your résumé that you've had lots of experience in the IT area. As a matter of fact you have a pretty impressive résumé.

Interviewee: Thanks. I've been in the IT area for quite a long time.

Interviewer: And what made you decide to study IT at college?

Interviewee: Well, I've always been into computers. I started using them when I was just 6-years-old and haven't stopped since then. I would spend hours surfing the web as a kid. My nickname at high school was the geek, you know, the computer geek. I guess I could really define myself as a computer freak, if you will.

Interviewer: Interesting. To be honest, computers have never been my strength and I don't really know much about information technology, but I admire people who do. So, how do you think you could use all your expertise in the area to help our company?

Interviewee: Well, for a start I'd have to get to know in detail how you do things in your company so I could figure out how IT would be at best service. I'm talking about all the computer systems and software that you are currently using and hardware as well. Do you know how many different systems you have in the company?

Interviewer: We have basically one system for each of the departments, that is, marketing and sales, administrative, financial and human resources. Four of them, I guess, but we can talk to our IT manager to check that out later. If I understood you correctly you mean you would redesign our IT department altogether after a thorough evaluation?

Interviewee: That's precisely it!

Interviewer: And would that mean we'd be saving money with all this reengineering in the long run?

Interviewee: That's quite possible. I've done that in two companies I worked for in the past, but that would not be all. You would certainly speed up many of your processes in the company as well.

Interviewer: That sounds really interesting. Would that imply a big investment in hardware and software?

Interviewee: Not necessarily. In many cases we can upgrade some of your current programs and improve others as well. By the way, do you have an intranet?

Interviewer: No, we don't. We thought about having one, though. But tell me, how do you envisage working with us? Would you consider working as a part-time freelance consultant?

Interviewee: Oh, definitely. I like being in touch with different companies and jobs at the same time. I'm pretty much a multitasker and like to be on the move.

Interviewer: Very good. I believe we should now set up a meeting with the presence of our IT manager so we could go into details about the department.

Interviewee: That would be perfect! Thank you.

VOCABULARY & EXPRESSIONS 12 - CAREER IN INFORMATION TECHNOLOGY

Right off the bat: immediately.
Take pride in: do something carefully and well.
Impressive: outstanding; remarkable.
I've always been into computers: I've always enjoyed computers a lot.
Geek (inf.): someone who is not popular because they do strange things or do not know how to behave in social situations; nerd.
Computer freak (inf.): someone who is extremely interested in computers.
Expertise: natural or acquired proficiency in a particular activity; ability; skill. » Veja "competência" p. 70
Software: computer programs.

Hardware: the physical and electronic parts of a computer.

To redesign/redesigned/redesigned: to recreate and work out the details of.

Altogether: completely; entirely.

Thorough: detailed; complete.

Precisely: exactly.

Reengineering: change of structure of an activity so that it performs better. » Veja "reengenharia" p. 96

In the long run: later in the future.

To speed up/sped up/sped up: to make something move or happen faster.

Intranet: a computer network used for exchanging information within a company. » Veja "intranet" p. 86

To envisage/envisaged/envisaged: to imagine or expect as a likely or desirable possibility in the future; to have a mental picture of.

Part-time: involving or working less than customary or standard hours. » Veja "meio período; de meio expediente (adj.); em meio expediente (adv.)" p. 89

Freelance: working independently for different companies rather than as an employee of a particular one. » Veja "freelance" p. 82

Definitely: absolutely; doubtlessly.

Multitasker: a person who does several things at the same time.

On the move: busy and active; traveling from one place to another.

Set up a meeting: arrange a meeting; schedule a meeting.

2. KEY JOB INTERVIEW QUESTIONS
Perguntas-chave de entrevista de emprego

Esta seção apresenta um roteiro com as 97 perguntas de entrevistas de emprego mais relevantes e freqüentes. Observe que cada pergunta pode ser feita de várias formas diferentes; por isso, tomamos o cuidado de agrupar perguntas similares logo abaixo da pergunta principal. Incluímos também perguntas que, de algum modo, estão relacionadas ao assunto tratado no grupo.

Se você possui um nível de conhecimento pós-intermediário do idioma, procure ouvir o áudio sem o apoio da leitura. Caso o seu nível esteja abaixo do intermediário, você pode utilizar o roteiro abaixo como suporte. Lembre-se de treinar a compreensão auditiva e preparar-se antecipadamente para responder as perguntas que podem surgir durante uma entrevista. Desse modo, você ficará mais autoconfiante e, certamente, irá melhorar o seu desempenho.

ılı|l|ı TRACK 13

1. **Tell me a little about yourself.**
   Conte-me um pouco sobre você.
1A. **How would you describe yourself?**
   Como você se descreveria?
1B. **What kind of adjectives would you use to describe yourself?**
   Quais adjetivos você usaria para se descrever?
1C. **How would you describe your personality?**
   Como você descreveria sua personalidade?
1D. **How would your co-workers describe you?**
   Como os seus colegas de trabalho descreveriam você?
1E. **What are your strengths and weaknesses in your opinion?**
   Quais são os seus pontos fortes e seus pontos fracos na sua opinião?

ılı|l|ı TRACK 14

2. **Why do you want to work for this organization?**
   Por que você quer trabalhar nesta empresa?
2A. **Why do you want this job?**
   Por que você quer este emprego?
2B. **Why would you like to work with us?**
   Por que você gostaria de trabalhar conosco?

2C. Why did you decide to seek a position in this company?
Por que você decidiu pleitear um cargo nesta empresa?

2D. What attracted you to this company?
O que atraiu você para esta empresa?

2E. What interests you about our product or service?
Por que você acha nosso produto ou serviço interessante?

2F. What do you know about our company?
O que você sabe sobre a nossa empresa?

2G. What do you know about our competitors?
O que você sabe sobre nossos concorrentes?

ıı|ı|ıı TRACK 15

3. How do you think you can contribute to our organization?
Como você acha que pode contribuir com a nossa empresa?

3A. In what ways do you think you can make a contribution to our organization?
De que forma você acha que pode contribuir com a nossa empresa?

3B. What makes you qualified for this position?
O que torna você qualificado para este cargo?

3C. What unique skills or knowledge can you contribute to our company?
Com quais habilidades ou conhecimento diferenciados você pode contribuir com a nossa empresa?

3D. Can you tell me a little about your experience in this area?
Você poderia me contar um pouco sobre sua experiência nesta área?

3E. What kind of background do you have?
Que tipo de formação você tem?

3F. Why should we hire you?
Por que nós deveríamos te contratar?

3G. Why should we select you over the other candidates?
Por que nós deveríamos escolher você e não os outros candidatos?

3H. What makes you believe you'd be ideal for this position?
O que faz você crer que você seria ideal para este cargo?

3I. Why did you choose a career in this area/field?
Por que você escolheu uma carreira nesta área?

3J. What qualities should a successful manager possess?
Quais são as qualidades que um gerente de sucesso deve ter?

ılılı• **TRACK 16**

4. **What are your short and long term career goals?**
   Quais são os seus objetivos profissionais a curto e médio prazo?
4A. **What do you expect to be doing five/ten years from now?**
   O que você espera estar fazendo daqui a cinco/dez anos?
4B. **What do you see yourself doing five/ten years from now?**
   O que você se vê fazendo daqui a cinco/dez anos?
4C. **How do you see yourself professionally five/ten years from now?**
   Como você se vê profissionalmente daqui a cinco/dez anos?

ılılı• **TRACK 17**

5. **Why do you want to leave your current job?**
   Por que você quer deixar o seu emprego atual?
5A. **Why did you quit your last job?**
   Por que você deixou seu último emprego?
5B. **Why did you leave your previous position?**
   Por que você deixou o seu cargo anterior?
5C. **Why did you decide to resign from your previous job?**
   Por que você decidiu pedir demissão de seu emprego anterior?
5D. **Why were you fired?**
   Por que você foi despedido?
5E. **How would you describe your present/previous boss?**
   Como você descreveria o seu chefe atual/anterior?
5F. **Who did you report to?**
   Para quem você se reportava?
5G. **What was it like working for your supervisor/boss?**
   Como era trabalhar para o seu supervisor/chefe?
5H. **Did you get along well with all the other co-workers?**
   Você tinha um bom relacionamento com todos os outros colegas de trabalho?

ılılı• **TRACK 18**

6. **What were your responsibilities in your last job?**
   Quais eram as suas responsabilidades no seu emprego anterior?
6A. **What are the most difficult decisions to make in your opinion?**
   Quais decisões você acha mais difíceis de tomar?
6B. **Describe a typical work day at your previous job.**
   Descreva um dia típico de trabalho no seu emprego anterior.

6C. How many hours did you normally work at your previous job?
Quantas horas você normalmente trabalhava em seu emprego anterior?

6D. Did you ever work overtime?
Você alguma vez fez hora extra?

6E. What did you like the most about your former job?
O que você mais gostava no seu emprego anterior?

6F. Tell me something you didn't like about your last job.
Me fale sobre algo que você não gostava em relação ao seu último emprego.

ılıılı· **TRACK 19**

7. What kind of activities do you find motivating?
Que tipos de atividades você acha motivadoras?

7A. What motivates you?
O que te motiva?

7B. Which work activities do you enjoy the most and the least?
De que atividades de trabalho você gosta mais e menos?

7C. Do you find any activities boring?
Você considera alguma atividade enfadonha/chata?

7D. What kind of thing bothers you the most at work?
Que tipo de coisa te incomoda mais no trabalho?

ılıılı· **TRACK 20**

8. How do you feel about teamwork?
Qual a sua opinião sobre trabalho em equipe?

8A. Do you prefer working in teams or alone?
Você prefere trabalhar em equipe ou sozinho?

8B. Can you delegate work?
Você sabe delegar trabalho?

8C. Are you good at delegating tasks?
Você é bom em delegar tarefas?

8D. What types of tasks can be delegated?
Que tipos de tarefas podem ser delegadas?

8E. What benefits does a supervisor receive from delegating work to employees?
Quais benefícios um supervisor tem ao delegar trabalho para os funcionários?

8F. In what kind of work environment are you most comfortable with?
Em que tipo de ambiente de trabalho você se sente mais à vontade?

ılıl||ı **TRACK 21**

9. **Describe the biggest challenge you've had at work and how you handled it.**
   Descreva o maior desafio que você teve no trabalho e como você lidou com o assunto.
9A. **Have you ever had a difficult situation at work? How did you deal with it?**
   Você já teve de enfrentar alguma situação difícil no trabalho? Como você lidou com ela?
9B. **Describe a situation where you had to work with a difficult person. What steps did you take to build a better relationship?**
   Descreva uma situação em que você precisou trabalhar com uma pessoa difícil. Quais atitudes você tomou para construir um melhor relacionamento?
9C. **What kind of people you don't usually get along with?**
   Com que tipo de pessoa você geralmente não se dá bem?
9D. **How have you dealt with conflict in the past?**
   Você já teve que lidar com conflitos no passado? Qual foi sua atitude?

ılıl||ı **TRACK 22**

10. **How do you handle stress?**
   Como você lida com o estresse?
10A. **How do you deal with stress and deadlines?**
   Como você lida com o estresse e com prazos/datas-limite?
10B. **What kind of situation makes you feel stressed?**
   Que tipo de situação faz você sentir-se estressado?
10C. **How do you work under pressure?**
   Como você reage ao trabalhar sobre pressão?
10D. **Can you work under pressure?**
   Você consegue trabalhar sobre pressão?
10E. **Do you consider yourself a workaholic?**
   Você se considera um workaholic?
10F. **What do you usually do to relax/unwind?**
   O que você geralmente faz para relaxar?
10G. **What do you like to do in your free time/spare time?**
   O que você gosta de fazer no seu tempo livre?
10H. **What do you like to do for fun?**
   O que você gosta de fazer para se divertir?
10I. **What are your favorite leisure time activities?**
   Quais são as suas atividades favoritas de lazer?

🔊 TRACK 23

11. **Did you have to travel a lot on business at your previous job?**
Você tinha que viajar muito a negócios no seu último emprego?
11A. **How often did you have to travel on business at your previous job?**
Com que freqüência você tinha que viajar a negócios no seu último emprego?
11B. **Do you mind traveling on business?**
Você se importa de viajar a negócios?
11C. **Would traveling on business be a problem for you?**
Viajar a negócios seria um problema para você?
11D. **Are you willing to travel?**
Você está disposto a viajar?
11E. **Are you willing to relocate?**
Você está disposto a se mudar?

🔊 TRACK 24

12. **Tell me about your accomplishments and failures in your previous job.**
Conte-me sobre as suas conquistas e fracassos no seu emprego anterior.
12A. **What was the biggest accomplishment in your previous job?**
Qual foi a sua maior conquista no seu emprego anterior?
12B. **What was the biggest failure in your previous job? What did you learn from it?**
Qual foi o seu maior fracasso no seu emprego anterior? O que você aprendeu com ele?
12C. **What accomplishments have given you the most satisfaction?**
Quais conquistas lhe deram maior satisfação?
12D. **What are your goals for the next five/ten years?**
Quais são os seus objetivos para os próximos cinco/dez anos?

🔊 TRACK 25

13. **What do you expect from this position?**
O que você espera deste cargo?
13A. **What are your expectations about this job?**
Quais são suas expectativas em relação a este emprego?
13B. **What are your salary expectations?**
Qual a sua expectativa em relação a salário?
13C. **What kind of salary are you expecting?**
Qual a sua expectativa em relação a salário?
13D. **What are your salary requirements (both short-term and long-term)?**
Quais são as suas necessidades quanto a salário, a curto e longo prazo?

13E. What were your starting and final levels of compensation at your previous job?
Qual foi o seu salário inicial e final no seu emprego anterior?

13F. What do you expect to be earning in five years?
Quanto você espera estar ganhando em cinco anos?

⑴⑴⑴ **TRACK 26**

14. How soon can you start?
Quando você pode começar?

14A. When can you start?
Quando você pode começar?

14B. Are you available to start immediately?
Você tem disponibilidade para começar imediatamente?

⑴⑴⑴ **TRACK 27**

15. Would you like to ask any questions? » Veja Interviewee's questions p. 47
Você gostaria de fazer alguma pergunta?

15A. Do you have any questions for me?
Você tem alguma pergunta para mim?

15B. Is there anything I haven't told you about the job or the company that you would like to know?
Tem alguma coisa que não te contei sobre o emprego ou a empresa, e que você gostaria de saber?

15C. Is there anything I haven't covered that you would like to know?
Há algo que não falei que você gostaria de perguntar?

3. SAMPLE ANSWERS TO
KEY JOB INTERVIEW QUESTIONS
Respostas-modelo às perguntas-chave de entrevista de emprego

Esta seção traz modelos de respostas para as perguntas mais comuns e relevantes em entrevistas de emprego. É importante enfatizar que os modelos apresentados são apenas exemplos e sugestões a partir dos quais você poderá moldar as suas próprias respostas.

A principal finalidade desta seção é preparar você para as perguntas-chave, de tal modo que você possa pensar previamente no que deseja responder e planejar as suas respostas com o auxílio do **Portuguese-English Glossary** p. 63.

Uma sugestão para você melhorar o seu desempenho e adquirir confiança é fazer simulações. Se você tem um colega que fale bem o idioma, peça a ele para que lhe faça as perguntas, de modo que você possa respondê-las em voz alta.

1. **Tell me a little about yourself.**
1A. How would you describe yourself?
1B. What kind of adjectives would you use to describe yourself?
1C. How would you describe your personality?
1D. How would your co-workers describe you?
1E. What are your strengths and weaknesses in your opinion?

1. I have over seven years of customer service experience. In this time, I have developed strong skills in customer care, troubleshooting and communication. Some of my strengths are getting the best out of people, multitasking and setting and achieving goals.

I was born and bred in... / I grew up in... / I've always lived in...

I started to work in advertising/insurance/etc. right after I finished college.

I'm... (procure no glossário p. 63 os traços de personalidade e habilidades que quer mencionar)

1A 1B 1C. I'm... (procure no glossário p. 63 os traços de personalidade e habilidades que quer mencionar)

I would say I'm hard working, focused and committed.

Well, I'm a very energetic person and I'm always willing to do the best I can in every situation.

1D. I guess my co-workers would say I'm... (procure no glossário p. 63 os traços de personalida-de e habilidades que quer mencionar)

1E. I have a strong ability to solve problems and build trust with clients. In many cases, I have had to work under very stressful situations, where I was able to handle with clarity and with a calm mind.

I would say my biggest weakness at my last job was that I had a hard time delegating. I would always want to do all job tasks, but this would cause me to not do as good a job as I would have liked. After noticing my job quality diminishing, I then started delegating tasks to my staff and the quality of our division increased quite well.

2. Why do you want to work for this organization?
2A. Why do you want this job?
2B. Why would you like to work with us?
2C. Why did you decide to seek a position in this company?
2D. What attracted you to this company?
2E. What interests you about our product or service?
2F. What do you know about our company?
2G. What do you know about our competitors?

2 2A 2B 2C 2D. Your company has shown its devotion to great customer service and quality. These are values that I share. Also, your company gives a lot back to the worker and seems to devote a lot to quality of life in the workplace. Because your company is growing each year, there are a lot of challenges to be met. Since I thrive on these types of challenges, I think that would be a great fit for me.

I am quite excited about the direction your company is moving in the international markets. I feel my last 7 years of experience has prepared me to take on many of these challenges.

I've always heard only good things from the people who work at your company. Besides that you are one of the market leaders in your field, so no doubt it would be great to work here.

Your company's reputation is definitely something that attracted me to it. I've always thought that working for a serious company that cares about its employees would be great.

2E. I think it would be great to work for a company whose products are highly considered in the market. Besides having a leading position in the market I know that you take good care of your employees.

2F. I know that your company has been expanding into international markets and thus the customer care division has increased its workload in a positive way. Because of an increase in sales, there has been an increase in after-sales customer service. I do think that I can help in that role.

2G. I know you have two main competitors, which also specialize in the same industry as you, but I'm also aware that you have a leading position and a very good reputation since your products are highly considered in the market.

3.   How do you think you can contribute to our organization?
3A. In what ways do you think you can make a contribution to our organization?
3B. What makes you qualified for this position?
3C. What unique skills or knowledge can you contribute to our company?
3D. Can you tell me a little about your experience in this area?
3E. What kind of background do you have?
3F. Why should we hire you?
3G. Why should we select you over the other candidates?
3H. What makes you believe you'd be ideal for this position?
3I. Why did you choose a career in this area/field?
3J. What qualities should a successful manager possess?

3 3A I feel that with all my managerial skills and experience I could definitely contribute in many ways. Besides that I have a proven track record in this business/industry and am a responsible, dedicated and reliable professional.

3B I have over seven years of experience in which I have advanced through many challenging levels of the profession. I have extensive experiences with problem solving, creative solutions that have increased sales and training and working with different types of people. I also can speak 3 languages and have lived overseas for 2 years, which I feel could give me an advantage in the international market.

I guess that besides having a proven track record in this field, the fact that I'm a dedicated and energetic person makes a big difference.

3C I believe the expertise I have developed over the years in this specific industry would enable me to contribute to your company. I have basically worked in all the areas of the industry and am familiar with all the processes involved.

3D Well, I have been working in this segment for over five years already and have had the chance to go through lots of experiences in this field. Apart from that I have always kept updated on the latest trends by attending seminars, conferences and courses.

3E As you must have seen in my résumé I graduated in mechanical engineering and I'm currently doing a master's in business administration, as I feel it would greatly enhance my professional skills.

3F 3G 3H Well, I guess I would have to say that apart from being qualified for the position and familiar with all the tasks involved, I'm a hard-working, dedicated and committed employee.

In my seven years of experience, I have been able to attain a strong foundation of knowledge and skills in the customer care field. Besides that I'm dedicated and reliable and I'm really willing to face new challenges.

3I I think the main reason is because I've always liked working with people and helping them solve their problems. I was also interested in incorporating these skills into a business environment. I felt that combining the love of creating better solutions for clients and people with practical business practices would fit me the best.

3J Apart from excellent interpersonal skills, I believe a successful manager should have the ability to organize and motivate his staff and also be supportive and help them with whatever needs they might have.

I think a successful manager should be... (procure no glossário p. 63 os traços de personalidade e habilidades que quer mencionar)

4. **What are your short and long term career goals?**
4A. What do you expect to be doing five/ten years from now?
4B. What do you see yourself doing five/ten years from now?
4C. How do you see yourself professionally five/ten years from now?

4 4A 4B 4C I would like to have a complete level of expertise in the sales and marketing arena which would enable me to head a complete division in a company such as yours.

Since I've been in this field for over five years and have had the chance to go through lots of experiences in this industry I feel that I'm really ready to face new challenges and earn a management position. As for long term I would definitely like to work my way up to becoming a director eventually.

Since you are moving into international business, I would like to see myself managing customer care service throughout an entire international region.

5. Why do you want to leave your current job?
5A. Why did you quit your last job?
5B. Why did you leave your previous position?
5C. Why did you decide to resign from your previous job?
5D. Why were you fired?
5E. How would you describe your present/previous boss?
5F. Who did you report to?
5G. What was it like working for your supervisor/boss?
5H. Did you get along well with all the other co-workers?

5 The opening at your company would be a great career move for me and present some new exciting challenges that I feel my current job does not have to offer.

5A 5B 5C I had a great opportunity to learn and develop professionally at my previous job. After having the chance to go through lots of experiences during the six years I worked there I felt I needed more challenges to develop my potential further. I really wanted to have more responsibility and new opportunities, which unfortunately were limited at my previous job because of the company size and their limited product line.

5D The company I worked for merged with a bigger one and as a consequence many positions were made redundant.

The company I worked for downsized as a result of a crisis it went through. About one third of its workforce was laid off.

5E I would have to say he's professional, committed and supportive, always willing to help his staff.

He's... (procure no glossário p. 63 os traços de personalidade e habilidades que quer mencionar)

5F I reported to the financial director. We used to have a quick daily meeting to talk about the on-going projects. We had a very good professional relationship.

5G It was really good. We got along really well. He would always make sure we understood what needed to be done and was quite supportive as well.

5H I did. All of the people working in my department were really friendly and nice and I can really say I had a good relationship with all of them.

6. **What were your responsibilities in your last job?**
6A. What are the most difficult decisions to make in your opinion?
6B. Describe a typical work day at your previous job.
6C. How many hours did you normally work at your previous job?
6D. Did you ever work overtime?
6E. What did you like the most about your former job?
6F. Tell me something you didn't like about your last job.

6 I was in charge of the IT department so one of my daily responsibilities was to supervise and delegate tasks to my staff. We had to make sure all the systems were running smoothly and solve any problems when they did occur.

I was responsible for customer support. I had a team of fifteen people under my supervision and we had to make sure we provided all our customers with information and other special needs. That also included taking care of disgruntled clients sometimes.

6A Well, definitely the ones that involve big investment. At my previous job we always tried to be extra careful to make sure we invested the company money wisely.

6B We used to have a daily meeting to discuss on-going projects and talk about any relevant subjects. As the sales manager I sometimes would also take the opportunity of the meeting to assign members of my staff with tasks that needed to be performed during the week. My typical work day also included following up on our salesmen's quotations and visits to clients.

6C I usually worked about 8 hours at my previous job. Sometimes when I needed to get something finished, like a report or something, I would stay late.

6D I didn't usually need to work overtime, but it did happen a couple of times.

6E I guess one of the things that I liked the most was the friendly environment. The people I worked with were really nice.

6F I lived quite far from the company so it took me a long time to get to work. This was definitely something I didn't like about my last job.

7. **What kind of activities do you find motivating?**
7A. What motivates you?
7B. Which work activities do you enjoy the most and the least?
7C. Do you find any activities boring?
7D. What kind of thing bothers you the most at work?
7 7A 7B I really like challenging activities when I can put into practice all my managerial skills.

Also trouble-shooting has always been something I've enjoyed a lot at the workplace.

Having goals to achieve is something that I find motivating.

I love working with people, you know, establishing goals and pushing them to do their best to achieve them. Of course that also means helping them out during the process. Something I honestly don't like very much is long meetings. But I know that is part of the process, so I always try to make them as productive as possible.

7C When an activity turns out to be boring I usually try to think of a different and more productive way of performing it.

7D I guess the thing that bothers me the most at work is when people are careless about their jobs or not really committed to them. That can really be a big problem since you depend on everybody's cooperation to achieve goals.

8. How do you feel about teamwork?
8A. Do you prefer working in teams or alone?
8B. Can you delegate work?
8C. Are you good at delegating tasks?
8D. What types of tasks can be delegated?
8E. What benefits does a supervisor receive from delegating work to employees?
8F. In what kind of work environment are you most comfortable with?

8 8A I like both teamwork and working alone as well. Depending on the job to be done, I sometimes feel that it can be more productive if you focus on it and do it by yourself, but no doubt teamwork is essential in many activities and to accomplish certain goals more rapidly and effectively.

8B 8C I wasn't very good at delegating tasks when I first started to work, but I had to learn how to do it so I could be more productive and it has certainly helped me in many ways.

8D I think certain routine tasks that have to be performed on a regular basis can be delegated, I mean, as long as the person who is going to be in charge of them have been previously trained and know exactly what to do.

8E I think a supervisor is more in control and is even more productive when he knows how to properly delegate work to his team. I mean, he is the one who needs to worry about the big picture and that all the tasks involved are carried out properly so that the final goal is achieved. I believe it's also his job to keep his staff motivated.

8F I'm a flexible person, so I feel that most work environments suit me well. I enjoy being a team player when needed, but I also like working independently.

9. Describe the biggest challenge you've had at work and how you handled it.
9A. Have you ever had a difficult situation at work? How did you deal with it?
9B. Describe a situation where you had to work with a difficult person. What steps did you take to build a better relationship?
9C. What kind of people don't you usually get along with?
9D. How have you dealt with conflict in the past?

9 9A Four years ago, one of our largest client's shipment was accidentally sent to the wrong address. The problem was that they needed it within the next 2 days. I immediately had myself and someone from my staff research and find out why there had been a mistake and where the shipment was exactly. I was able to get the shipment sent again to the correct address and delivered in time with no extra cost to the client. While this was happening, I kept in contact with our client and assured them that we would get everything in order in a timely manner.

About two years ago at my previous company, we had an order for our most important client sent to the wrong address. It was our German client and they were quite angry to say the least. I was able to negotiate a new delivery date and coordinated a new shipment to be expedited immediately. After that happened I created a better after-sales service that produced a lot of positive feedback from our clients.

9B I've never really had any serious problems working with anyone. I can get along with most people easily and I always try to understand different points of view.

Luckily I've never had a confrontational situation with a co-worker. I have had disagreements. My approach is always to listen to their needs and frustrations. The more you listen, the more you can "stand in their shoes". The more empathetic you can be. I feel it is a good way to demonstrate emotional intelligence.

9C I usually get along with most people without any problems, but if I had to tell you what kind of people I don't usually like, that would be snobbish, arrogant people.

9D I've never had to deal with strong conflict. Anyway, I believe in open communication and my door is always open. I believe in listening and being empathetic. It has always worked for me so far.

10. How do you handle stress?
10A. How do you deal with stress and deadlines?
10B. What kind of situation makes you feel stressed?
10C. How do you work under pressure?
10D. Can you work under pressure?
10E. Do you consider yourself a workaholic?
10F. What do you usually do to relax/unwind?
10G. What do you like to do in your free time/spare time?
10H. What do you like to do for fun?
10I. What are your favorite leisure time activities?

10 10A 10B 10C 10D Being in customer care is quite stressful as you know. So when I am at work, I do try to take time to step away from my desk or phone and do some breathing exercises or stretch. I always find these habits work. I also make sure to leave the work problems at the office and concentrate on my family at home.

I find that working out at the gym helps me cope with the everyday stress and pressure at work. I really feel like a brand-new person after a good workout.

10E I wouldn't say so. I mean, I do like to work hard and try to always do my best, but I also think it's important to have some time to relax. I even feel that being a workaholic is in fact counter-productive.

Well, my friends often say I am a workaholic. I would say I am just over-zealous about anything that is work-related.

10F 10G 10H 10I I like to spend time with my wife and kids. We usually go to parks and travel to the countryside on weekends. I find it really relaxing and it does recharge my batteries.

Apart from spending time with my family I enjoy going to the club to do some physical exercise, meet my friends, watch comedy shows and read.

11. Did you have to travel a lot on business at your previous job?
11A. How often did you have to travel on business at your previous job?
11B. Do you mind traveling on business?
11C. Would traveling on business be a problem for you?
11D. Are you willing to travel?
11E. Are you willing to relocate?

11 11A Not very often, about once a month.

I used to travel about once a week. Very short trips. In some cases, I would catch an early morning flight and be back home on the same day.

11B 11C Not at all! I actually enjoy traveling on business. I find it stimulating and it does break up the routine.

11D Sure! I would definitely be willing to travel. I actually enjoy business trips.

Well, to be honest, traveling on business would be okay as long as it didn't imply staying away from my family for many days.

11E I would certainly consider it a possibility. I have lived in other places before and really enjoyed the experience.

Well, I would have to think carefully about it, I mean, that's a decision that would also affect my family, you know, it's not just a personal thing. To be perfectly honest with you, moving somewhere else is not something I would enjoy doing, really.

12. Tell me about your accomplishments and failures in your previous job.
12A. What was the biggest accomplishment in your previous job?
12B. What was the biggest failure in your previous job? What did you learn from it?
12C. Which accomplishments have given you the most satisfaction?
12D. What are your goals for the next five/ten years?

12 12A 12B Two years ago at my previous company, I implemented a new customer care system that better streamlined the process of before and after-sales service. We received feedback from our customers that the new service had given us a more caring image. Because of this, our sales increased by 26% that year and it was believed to relate directly to the new implemented service. That was definitely the accomplishment that gave me the most satisfaction. One of my biggest failures was not to be able to delegate work properly. That was something I had to learn how to do and I do feel it has made me more productive in many ways.

12C Nothing satisfies me more than seeing that the customer gets the absolutely best service that we can provide. This is always a challenge and I thrive the best from this.

12D I've been in this field for about nine years now and have had the chance to go through lots of experiences, so I feel that I'm ready to for new challenges and to take on new responsibilities. One of my short-term goals is to earn a management position.

I plan to continue to work hard and develop professionally and eventually become a manager/ director

13. What do you expect from this position?
13A. What are your expectations about this job?
13B. What are your salary expectations?
13C. What kind of salary are you expecting?
13D. What are your salary requirements (both short-term and long-term)?
13E. What were your starting and final levels of compensation at your previous job?
13F. What do you expect to be earning in five years?

13 13A I see it as a great opportunity for me to put into practice all the skills I have acquired in the past few years. I'm also excited about the challenges that the position would definitely pose and I really feel I could learn a lot and grow, both professionally and personally.

13B 13C I would be expecting to have an initial salary of about $ 8,000 monthly which would be just a little over what I was making at my previous job.

13D To start with, I would need to make at least a little over what I was making at my previous job. I would definitely be expecting to make more as I work hard and develop professionally.

13E When I first started at XYZ company my salary was $ 5,000 monthly. Two years later, it increased by 20% and my last paycheck there, I mean, a year after this increase, was for $ 7,000 monthly.

13F To be honest I haven't really thought about it, I mean I would certainly expect to be making more than now, but I also know that will depend on how hard I work, my commitment to the company and a lot of other aspects.

14. How soon can you start?
14A. When can you start?
14B. Are you available to start immediately?

14 I'm available to start immediately.

I could start as soon as you need me.

14A I believe I would just need a couple of weeks to work some things out, but I could definitely start very soon.

14B Definitely. I'd be glad to.

Sure, I'd love to!

15. **Would you like to ask any questions?** » Veja Interviewee's questions p. 47

15A. Do you have any questions for me? » Veja Interviewee's questions p. 47

15B. Is there anything I haven't told you about the job or the company that you would like to know? » Veja Interviewee's questions p. 47

15C. Is there anything I haven't covered that you would like to know? » Veja Interviewee's questions p. 47

4. INTERVIEWEE'S QUESTIONS
Perguntas do entrevistado

É natural que, durante uma entrevista, você também queira fazer perguntas. Isso acontece como resultado natural da interação. Em muitos casos, o próprio entrevistador dará a você uma oportunidade para fazer perguntas sobre o cargo pretendido e a empresa. De qualquer modo, lembre-se sempre de que é você o entrevistado. Por isso, evite ser impertinente.

Contanto que você aguarde o momento oportuno, fazer perguntas ao entrevistador é uma atitude bem vista, pois mostra seu interesse pelo cargo e pela empresa. Além disso, é uma ótima maneira de descobrir se a empresa e o cargo oferecido realmente combinam com você e estão dentro de suas expectativas.

ᵢ₁₁ᵢ TRACK 28

1. **What are the day-to-day responsibilities of this job?**
   Quais são as responsabilidades diárias desta função?

2. **What are some of the skills and abilities necessary for someone to succeed in this job?**
   Quais são as habilidades necessárias para desempenhar esta função com sucesso?

3. **Is this a new position?**
   Este cargo é novo?

4. **What particular computer equipment and software do you use?**
   Quais equipamentos de informática e softwares vocês usam?

5. **Who will review my performance? How often?**
   Quem vai avaliar o meu desempenho? Com que freqüência?

6. **Who does this position report to?**
   Este cargo reporta a quem?

7. **Could you explain your organizational structure?**
   Você poderia explicar o organograma da empresa?

8. **How many people work in this office/department?**
   Quantas pessoas trabalham neste escritório/departamento?

9. **Does the job require a lot of traveling?**
   É preciso viajar muito nesta função?

10. **Is relocation a possibility?**
    É possível ter que mudar de cidade?

11. **What is your organization's policy on transfers to other cities?**
    Qual é a política da empresa com relação a transferências para outras cidades?

12. **What are the hours like?**
    Qual é o horário de trabalho?

13. **What is the typical work day? Is overtime expected?**
    Como é um dia típico de trabalho? É comum ter de fazer hora-extra?

14. **What are the prospects for growth and advancement?**
    Qual é a perspectiva de crescimento e promoções?

15. **What about career plan, does the company offer promotion opportunities?**
    E com relação a plano de carreira, a empresa oferece oportunidades de promoção?

16. **What kind of work can I expect to be doing the first year?**
    Que tipo de trabalho eu devo fazer no primeiro ano?

17. **What kinds of benefits does the company provide?**
    Que tipo de benefícios a empresa oferece?

18. **How long a vacation are the employees entitled to?**
    A quanto tempo de férias os funcionários têm direito?

19. **What is the organization's plan for the next five years, and how does this department fit in?**
    Quais são os planos da empresa para os próximos cinco anos, e como este departamento se encaixa neles?

20. **What would be the initial salary for this position?**
    Qual seria o salário inicial para este cargo?

21. **Does the company offer any training and development programs?**
    A empresa oferece programas de treinamento e desenvolvimento?

22. **What is the company's policy on providing seminars, workshops, and training so employees can keep up their skills or acquire new ones?**
Qual é a política da empresa quanto a seminários, workshops e treinamentos, de modo que os funcionários possam manter suas habilidades e adquirir outras?

23. **When would you expect me to start?**
Quando eu precisaria começar?

24. **If I am given a job offer, how soon would you like me to start?**
Se me oferecerem o emprego, quando vocês gostariam que eu começasse?

25. **When can I expect to hear from you?**
Quando eu provavelmente terei notícias de vocês?

26. **Would you like a list of references?**
Você gostaria de uma lista de referências?

27. **Are there any other questions I can answer for you?**
Há alguma outra pergunta que eu possa responder?

5. PRACTICE SETS
Exercícios práticos

PRACTICE SET 1

A. Fill in the blanks with an appropriate word/expression or verb from the box. Make sure you use the appropriate verb tense.

> volunteer work   maternity leave   employ   recruit   teamwork
> commitment   networking   tasks   proactive   résumé

1. "What types of _____ can be delegated in your opinion?", the interviewer asked the candidate.
2. "Could you please e-mail your _____ to us?", the human resources analyst told Claire over the phone.
3. This position requires someone with a _____ profile.
4. "Make sure you bring some business cards. We'll certainly do some _____ at the conference tomorrow", said Bill to a co-worker.
5. "In order to achieve our goals, _____ is essential", said the sales director at the meeting.
6. Many companies try to _____ at job fairs.
7. Doing _____ such as looking after elderly people or helping orphaned children can help enhance your life.
8. "We need to hire someone to fill in for Liz while she is away on _____", said Brian at the meeting.
9. How many people does that factory _____?
10. "We won't be able to reach the goals without everyone's _____", explained Mr. Clark at the meeting.

B. Choose the alternative that best explains the meaning of the words or expressions in the sentences below.

1. A dead-end job is...
(a) a job that is endless.
(b) a job that offers a good salary and a good chance of progress.
(c) a job with a low salary and no chance of progress.
(d) a job with good promotion and development opportunities.

51

2. **"The applicant wasn't hired because his résumé wasn't good enough", said the human resources manager.**
(a) the applicant was not hired because he was overqualified for the job.
(b) the applicant was not hired because he showed no interest in the job.
(c) the applicant was not hired because he was not qualified for the job.
(d) the applicant was not hired because the interviewer was unsure of his qualifications.

3. **"My evening commute takes about 30 minutes", Jeff told Mike. Jeff told Mike that...**
(a) It takes him about 30 minutes to go from work to his home in the evening.
(b) He walks his dog for about 30 minutes every evening.
(c) He walks on the treadmill for about 30 minutes in the evening in order to keep fit.
(d) He watches TV for about 30 minutes in the evening.

4. **A company's core business is...**
(a) a company's least important business or activity.
(b) a company's main business or activity.
(c) all the range of products sold by a company.
(d) a company's performance in the market place.

5. **If an employee gives notice or hands in his notice, he...**
(a) informs his employer about the recent market trends.
(b) lets his employer know beforehand that he will leave the job.
(c) keeps his boss posted on the progress of his work.
(d) briefs his boss on the latest market news.

C. **Match the words or expressions on the left (1-10) with the definitions below (a-j).**

1. mentor
2. to resign
3. deadline
4. outplacement
5. turnover
6. union
7. outsourcing
8. teamwork
9. seasonal work
10. shift

(a) working in a job where you are employed only at certain times of the year
(b) an organization formed by workers to protect their rights
(c) the combined actions of a group of people working together effectively to achieve a goal

(d) to officially announce that you have decided to leave your job or an organization

(e) the period that a person is scheduled to work, or a group of workers who work during the same period of time

(f) a service that a company provides to help its workers find new jobs when it cannot continue to employ them

(g) the rate at which employees leave a company and are replaced by others

(h) a time or day by which something must be done

(i) an experienced person who gives another person advice and help, esp. related to work

(j) when a company uses workers from outside the company to do a job

PRACTICE SET 2

A. Fill in the blanks with an appropriate word/expression or verb from the box. Make sure you use the appropriate verb tense.

> **hire   supervise   recruitment   break   profits**
> **interview   full-time   resign   turnover   shift**

1. The shareholders held a meeting to discuss the _____ for the last quarter.
2. "I think we all need a _____. Come on, let's have some coffee", said the manager to his staff.
3. The HR department is _____ three candidates for the job.
4. "Are you looking for a part-time job or a _____ job?", the interviewer asked Joan at the interview.
5. The company Brian works for has a very high _____ of staff.
6. We were all surprised to hear David _____ after being with the company for more than fifteen years.
7. Nick works on the night _____.
8. "As a manager I _____ a staff of 15 people", said Greg at the interview.
9. "We'll have to _____ more people and acquire new machines if demand for our products keeps up", the factory manager told Mike.
10. One of the job duties of HR is _____ of new workers.

B. Choose the alternative that best explains the meaning of the words or expressions in the sentences below.

1. When an employee has a day off, he or she...
(a) has a bad day at work.

53

(b) has a busy day at work.

(c) has a free day from work.

(d) has a good day at work.

2. **If someone works on a freelance basis, he or she...**

(a) works independently for different companies rather than being employed by one company.

(b) works from home, without commuting to work every day.

(c) is a regular employee at a company.

(d) does not need to report to anyone in the company.

3. **"The factory manager will have to hire new people to fill in for some workers who are away on sick leave." The factory manager will have to...**

(a) dismiss people since there are far too many employees.

(b) employ new people to substitute workers who are sick.

(c) fire some employees who have not been working properly.

(d) find out why the absenteeism rate has been increasing.

4. **If two companies merge, they...**

(a) join together so they can help each other financially.

(b) join together so they can beat the competition.

(c) join together to form one larger company.

(d) join together in order to reduce their overall expenses.

5. **"Many people don't need to commute to work anymore", because they...**

(a) think public transportation is not as good as it used to be.

(b) work from their home offices.

(c) travel a long distance to get to work.

(d) don't enjoy riding the subway to work.

C. **Match the words or expressions on the left (1-10) with the definitions below (a-j).**

1. to go on strike
2. to work overtime
3. trade show
4. branch office
5. merger
6. track record
7. maternity leave
8. sick leave
9. to commute
10. internship

(a) time that you are allowed to spend away from work because you are sick
(b) a job that lasts for a short time, that someone, esp. a student, does in order to gain experience
(c) all of a person's past achievements, successes or failures
(d) to travel regularly a distance between home and work
(e) time that a mother is allowed to spend away from work when she has a baby
(f) a big exhibition when several companies show their goods or services, to try to sell them
(g) the combining of two or more companies into one
(h) to stop working as a protest, ex. for a higher salary or better working conditions
(i) a local office that is part of a larger organization with a main office elsewhere
(j) to spend time working in your job in addition to your normal working hours

PRACTICE SET 3

A. Fill in the blanks with an appropriate word/expression or verb from the box. Make sure you use the appropriate verb tense.

> **shift   part-time   classified ads   overtime   seasonal work
> network   rapport   advertising campaign   outsourcing   brainstorming**

1. We always come up with lots of new ideas when we have a _____ session.
2. "If demand for our products keeps up we'll have to start thinking of a third _____", said the factory manager at the meeting.
3. It's always important to carry your business card in case you decide to _____.
4. "Let's schedule a meeting to talk about the _____ for the new product", Mr. Wilcox told Eliot.
5. "Why don't you take a look at the _____? You might find a good job opportunity", said Susan to a friend.
6. Gary is a friendly guy and has a very good _____ with all his co-workers.
7. Kim doesn't work all day long. She has a _____ job.
8. "Did you have to work _____ at your previous job?", the interviewer asked the candidate.
9. _____ of non-core activities is a usual practice among many companies nowadays.
10. Many American college students do _____ in the summer to save money for their classes.

B. Choose the alternative that best explains the meaning of the words or expressions in the sentences below.

1. "Networking is one of the most important things to do to find a job." Networking can be defined as...
(a) the practice of doing research on the Net to find out job opportunities.
(b) the practice of attending lectures with co-workers in order to improve one's skills.
(c) the practice of meeting other people involved in the same kind of work to exchange information.
(d) the practice of e-mailing one's résumé to many different companies.

2. The opposite meaning of the verbs employ, dismiss and manage (a business) is...
(a) hire, fire and run (a business)
(b) dismiss, fire and run (a business)
(c) fire, hire and run (a business)
(d) recruit, hire and run (a business)

3. "The salary is not that good, but the perks are great", said Bill to a friend. Bill told a friend...
(a) the salary is not so good but the possibility of growth is great.
(b) the salary could be better, but he is satisfied anyway.
(c) the salary is not so good, but he will be promoted soon.
(d) the salary is not so good, but the benefits are great.

4. "The sales department is short-staffed", Gary told the human resources manager. The company needs to...
(a) fire some employees in the sales department.
(b) find out who has not being doing their job properly in the sales department.
(c) hire more employees for the sales department.
(d) find out why they have not reached the sales goals.

5. "The absenteeism rate at the factory has been dropping in the past few months", said the factory manager. The factory manager said that...
(a) the number of factory workers on sick leave has been dropping.
(b) the number of absent workers has been reducing.
(c) the number of factory workers on sick leave has been increasing.
(d) the number of absent workers has been going up.

C. Match the words or expressions on the left (1-10) with the definitions below (a-j).

1. to give notice
2. to delegate
3. to fire
4. day off
5. entrepreneur
6. dead-end job
7. dot-com company
8. expertise
9. intern
10. labor

(a) to dismiss from employment
(b) special skill or knowledge in a particular subject
(c) to warn an employer that you are going to leave your job
(d) a company whose business is done using the Internet or involves the Internet
(e) someone, esp. a student, who works for a short time in a particular job in order to gain experience
(f) all the people who work for a company or in a country
(g) a 24-hour break from work
(h) to give a job or responsibility to someone in a lower position instead of doing it yourself
(i) a person who starts or runs a business activity, esp. one that involves financial risk
(j) a job with a low salary and no chance of progress

PRACTICE SET 4

A. Fill in the blanks with an appropriate word/expression or verb from the box. Make sure you use the appropriate verb tense.

internship	fringe benefits	day off	proactive	delegated
strengths	competitive edge	duties	freelance	staff

1. The company Roger works for employs a total of 57 _____.
2. Bill used to have a full-time job in the pharmaceutical industry, but now he works as a _____ consultant.
3. "One of my _____ at my previous job was to supervise the store clerks", said the applicant to the interviewer.
4. "They offer a company car and health insurance among other _____", said Ralph to a friend.

5. Certain types of tasks cannot be _____.
6. "What are your _____ and weaknesses in your opinion?", the interviewer asked Brian at the interview.
7. Doing an _____ is the best way of gaining practical job experience.
8. Tom is a _____ employee who enjoys responsibility and challenges.
9. "I like to go to the park and get a suntan on my _____", Jack told a co--worker.
10. Learning a second language can give you a _____ when looking for a job.

B. Choose the alternative that best explains the meaning of the words or expressions in the sentences below.

1. The best definition for outsourcing is...
(a) when a company closes down.
(b) when a company breaks even.
(c) when a company uses workers from outside the company to do a job.
(d) when a company downsizes its workforce.

2. If a company breaks even, it...
(a) neither makes a profit, nor loses money.
(b) starts making money hand over fist.
(c) goes bankrupt.
(d) closes down.

3. If someone does seasonal work, he or she...
(a) does voluntary work.
(b) works in a job where they are employed only at certain times of the year.
(c) does volunteer work.
(d) works in a job where the environmental conditions are appropriate.

4. If the employees of a factory go on strike, they...
(a) work overtime to meet production deadlines.
(b) increase production volume.
(c) go on a collective vacation.
(d) stop working as a protest, ex. for a higher salary or better working conditions.

5. If someone works part-time, he or she...
(a) works all day long.
(b) works day in, day out.
(c) does not commute to work every day.
(d) works less than customary or standard hours.

C. Match the words or expressions on the left (1-10) with the definitions below (a-j).

1. fringe benefits
2. opening
3. brainstorming
4. to retire
5. position
6. co-worker
7. benchmark
8. competitor
9. to hire
10. résumé

(a) summary of one's career and qualifications
(b) a standard for measuring or judging other things of the same type
(c) a person or company that offers the same goods or services as another and competes for the same customers
(d) to employ someone
(e) a person who works with you and has a similar position
(f) a job
(g) special advantages or benefits in addition to the salary you are paid
(h) a method of solving problems or planning activities in which all the members of a group make suggestions
(i) to end a career
(j) a job that is available

PRACTICE SET 5

A. Fill in the blanks with an appropriate word/expression or verb from the box. Make sure you use the appropriate verb tense.

> **absenteeism   core business   retire   benchmark   sample**
> **entrepreneur   employment agency   noticeboard   employees   retail**

1. "Why don't you check out an _____? They might have just the job for you", Ruth advised a friend.
2. That big company's procedures are a _____ for its competitors.
3. "Being an _____ is exciting because you are your own boss, but it is also quite time consuming", explained Roger to a friend.

4. Many companies buy wholesale and then sell in their store at a _____ price.
5. The _____ lists announcements regarding job openings and events in the company.
6. Frank plans to move to Florida when he _____.
7. "We have to find out why we've had so much _____ in the last two months", Bill told the factory manager.
8. Over two hundred _____ work at that big car plant.
9. Many companies prefer to concentrate on their _____ and outsource other departments.
10. "We need to see a _____ of the product before buying", said the purchasing manager at the meeting.

B. Choose the alternative that best explains the meaning of the words or expressions in the sentences below.

1. **"The company Brian works for has a very high turnover of staff." The best definition for turnover is...**
(a) clever and sophisticated.
(b) the rate at which employees leave a company and are replaced by others.
(c) confused and disorganized.
(d) the rate at which employees are promoted.

2. **Doing an internship is a good way to...**
(a) learn how to deal with disgruntled customers.
(b) prepare oneself for college tests.
(c) gain practical work experience.
(d) improve one's fitness.

3. **"The applicant we interviewed this morning has an outstanding résumé", said the human resources manager to her boss.**
(a) the applicant is probably experienced and qualified.
(b) the applicant is probably not qualified for the position available.
(c) the applicant has had international experience.
(d) the applicant's résumé has not been carefully checked so far.

4. **The factory workers have gone on strike for a raise in their salaries.**
(a) they have increased their production capacity.
(b) they stopped working for an increase in their salaries.
(c) they have been unhappy about the overall working conditions.
(d) they have been working overtime to meet the deadline.

5. **If a company outsources a department, it...**
(a) reduces the number of people working in the department.
(b) eliminates the department.
(c) increases the number of people working in the department.
(d) uses workers from outside the company to do the job of the department.

C. **Match the words or expressions on the left (1-10) with the definitions below (a-j).**

1. absenteeism
2. perks
3. to advertise
4. applicant
5. retiree
6. to attend
7. to take over
8. customer service
9. core business
10. competition

(a) someone who has stopped working, usually because of their age
(b) a person who formally requests a job; candidate
(c) to be present at an event (a meeting, a lecture, etc.) or go regularly to a place (school, church, etc.)
(d) additional advantages given with a job besides the salary
(e) frequent absence from work
(f) to make a product, a service, a job opportunity, etc. known to people
(g) a situation in which people or organizations try to be more successful than other people or organizations
(h) the main business or activities of a company
(i) the department of a company that deals with questions, problems, etc. that customers have
(j) to buy a company or gain control of it; to take control or responsibility for something, esp. in place of someone else

6. PORTUGUESE-ENGLISH GLOSSARY
Glossário Português-Inglês

A

Abono: veja "bônus" p. 68

Absenteísmo: absenteeism
» What's the absenteeism rate at the company you work for?
Qual é a taxa de absenteísmo na empresa em que você trabalha?
» "The absenteeism rate has been dropping in the past few months", the factory manager told a co-worker.
"A taxa de absenteísmo tem caído nos últimos meses", o gerente da fábrica disse a um colega de trabalho.

Acionista: shareholder
» "Were the shareholders pleased with the quarterly results?", asked Derek at the meeting.
"Os acionistas ficaram satisfeitos com os resultados do trimestre?", perguntou Derek na reunião.

Ações de empresa: shares
» "I was surprised to hear that George sold his shares of the company", Tom told Luke.
"Fiquei surpreso em saber que o George vendeu as ações dele na empresa", Tom disse a Luke.
» The news that Walter decided to sell his shares of the company spread quickly.
A notícia de que Walter decidiu vender suas ações da empresa se espalhou rapidamente.

Ações de mercado: stocks
» Investing in stocks can be risky even if you are familiar with the stock market.
Investir em ações pode ser arriscado, mesmo se você estiver familiarizado com o mercado de ações.

Adiantamento: an advance; an advance payment

Adquirir; comprar: to acquire/acquired/acquired
» "We have decided to acquire two new machines", the factory manager told a co-worker.
"Decidimos comprar mais duas máquinas novas", o gerente da fábrica disse a um colega de trabalho.

Advogado(a): lawyer; attorney

Afinidade; entrosamento; bom relacionamento: rapport

» Mike has always had an excellent rapport with all his co-workers.
Mike sempre teve um excelente relacionamento com todos os colegas de trabalho.

Agência de empregos: employment agency

Agenda; pauta: agenda

» "... and the next item on the agenda is – Boosting sales, quarterly goals", said Frank at the meeting.
"... e o próximo item em pauta é – Aumentando as vendas, metas trimestrais", disse Frank durante a reunião.

Agregar valor: to add value

» "We should focus on what really adds value to our business", said Mr. Clark at the meeting.
"Precisamos nos concentrar naquilo que realmente agrega valor ao nosso negócio", disse o sr. Clark na reunião.

Agronomia: agronomy

Agrônomo: agronomist

Alta, aumento da atividade econômica: boom

» Many new job opportunities have been created thanks to the recent boom.
Muitas oportunidades novas de emprego foram criadas graças ao recente aumento da atividade econômica.

Amigável; simpático: friendly

» Ed is a very friendly co-worker.
O Ed é um colega de trabalho muito simpático.

Amostra: sample

» Could you please send us some samples of your products?
Você poderia, por favor, nos enviar algumas amostras de seus produtos?

Analista de sistemas: systems analyst

Anexar, incluir um anexo a uma mensagem de e-mail: to attach/attached/attached

» As per our conversation, please see the document attached.
Conforme nossa conversa, por favor veja o documento em anexo.

Anexo, documento enviado com um e-mail: attachment

» We can send Word and Excel documents as an attachment.
Podemos enviar documentos do Word e Excel em anexo.

Anunciar; fazer publicidade; divulgar: to advertise/advertised/advertised

» "How do you think we should advertise the new product?", asked Mike at the meeting.
"Como vocês acham que deveríamos divulgar o novo produto?", perguntou Mike na reunião.

Anúncio de emprego: job ad

» "If I were you I'd take a look at the job ads. You might find some interesting job opportunities", Clint advised a friend.
"Se eu fosse você daria uma olhada nos anúncios de emprego. Talvez você encontre alguma oportunidade de emprego interessante", Clint aconselhou um amigo.

Anúncios classificados: classified ads

» "I think I am going to take a look at the classified ads in the newspaper. I really need to find a new job", Karen told Ann.
"Acho que vou dar uma olhada nos anúncios classificados do jornal. Eu realmente preciso encontrar um novo emprego", Karen disse para Ann.

» "The best jobs are not usually advertised in the newspaper classified ads", Tim told a friend.
"Os melhores empregos geralmente não são anunciados nos classificados dos jornais", Tim disse a um amigo.

Aposentadoria: retirement

Aposentar-se: to retire/retired/retired

» Mr. Harrison will take over as general manager when Mr. Brown retires.
O Sr. Harrison vai assumir como gerente geral quando o Sr. Brown se aposentar.

Aposentado: retiree

Aquisição: acquisition

» "Their latest acquisition was a software business in Silicon Valley, California", said Frank at the meeting.
"A aquisição mais recente deles foi uma empresa de software no Vale do Silício, Califórnia", disse Frank na reunião.

Arquitetura: architecture

Arquiteto(a): architect

Arroba (em endereços de e-mail): at

» A: What's your e-mail address?
B: It's my name at my company dot com dot br (myname@mycompany.com.br)
A: Qual é o seu e-mail?
B: É meu nome arroba minha empresa ponto com ponto br (meunome@minhacompanhia.com.br).

Assistir (palestras, aulas etc.); participar, freqüentar (congressos, feiras de negócios, seminários etc.): to attend/attended/attended

» All the salesmen in our company are supposed to attend the sales seminars that are held twice a year.
Todos os vendedores na nossa empresa devem participar dos seminários de vendas que acontecem duas vezes por ano.

» I would have known what to do if I had attended the lecture.
Eu saberia o que fazer se tivesse assistido à palestra.

» Have you attended any trade shows lately?
Você participou de alguma feira comercial nos últimos tempos?

Assumir uma função: to take over/took over/taken over

» Mr. Drake took over as sales manager after Mr. Williams retired.
O Sr. Drake assumiu a função de gerente de vendas depois que o Sr. Williams se aposentou.

Atacado: wholesale. » Veja também "varejo" p. 101

» "I need a list with the wholesale price of all the products", the sales director told Mark.
"Preciso de uma lista com o preço de atacado de todos os produtos", o diretor de vendas disse para o Mark.

Atencioso(a): considerate

Atendimento ao cliente: customer service

» Brian has over five years of customer service experience.
Brian tem mais de cinco anos de experiência com atendimento ao cliente.

» Good customer service is the best way to keep your clients.
Um bom atendimento é a melhor forma de fidelizar seus clientes.

Atingir o ponto de equilíbrio; não ter lucro nem prejuízo; "empatar": to break even

» Most new businesses take at least a year to just break even.
A maioria dos novos negócios leva pelo menos um ano para apenas atingir o ponto de equilíbrio.

» It takes a couple of years to break even when you start your own business. Usually a start-up loses money for the first two years.

Leva alguns anos para atingir o ponto de equilíbrio quando se inicia um negócio próprio. Uma empresa iniciante geralmente perde dinheiro nos dois primeiros anos.

Atividade principal de uma empresa: core business

» **What's your company's core business?**
Qual é a atividade principal da sua empresa?

Atualizado: up-to-date; updated

» **A good professional should always keep updated.**
Um bom profissional deve manter-se sempre atualizado.

Auditor: auditor

» **"We'll have an auditor come in next week to check our accounting", said Walter at the meeting.**
"Um auditor virá na próxima semana para verificar a nossa contabilidade", Walter disse na reunião.

Auditoria: auditing

Auditar: to audit/audited/audited

» **They will be auditing the financial division of our company next week.**
A divisão financeira de nossa empresa será auditada na próxima semana.

Aumentar; desenvolver-se rapidamente: to boom/boomed/boomed

» **Sales of our product have been booming ever since the new director took over.**
As vendas dos nossos produtos têm aumentado bastante desde que o novo diretor assumiu o cargo.

» **The IT area boomed in Silicon Valley in the San Francisco Bay Area in the late 90's.**
O ramo de TI desenvolveu-se rapidamente no Vale do Silício, na região da Baía de San Francisco, no final da década de 1990.

Aumentar o preço: to mark up

» **Retailers usually buy their products wholesale and then they mark up the price to sell to the public.**
Os varejistas geralmente compram seus produtos no atacado e, então, aumentam o preço para vender ao público.

Aumento de preços: mark-up

» **"Our supplier made a mark-up on their product so we had to pay more", Gary explained to his co-workers.**
"Nosso fornecedor aumentou o preço de seu produto e, por isso, tivemos de pagar mais", Gary explicou aos colegas de trabalho.

Autoconfiante: self-assured; self-confident

Automotivado: self-motivated

Autônomo: self-employed

Autoritário(a); "mandão": bossy

» Many employees find it hard to put up with the new manager because of his bossy style.
Muitos funcionários acham difícil suportar o novo gerente por causa de seu estilo autoritário.

Aviso prévio: notice.   » Veja "dar aviso prévio" p. 73

B

Bancário(a): bank clerk

Banqueiro: banker

Benchmark: referencial de excelência

» The company Richard works for is considered a benchmark in the beverage industry.
A empresa para a qual Richard trabalha é considerada um referencial de excelência na indústria de bebidas.

» Nike is a benchmark for marketing and advertising in modern business.
A Nike é um referencial de excelência em marketing e propaganda no mundo corporativo.

Benefícios (além do salário): fringe benefits; perks (informal, "mordomia")

» What kind of fringe benefits does the company you work for offer their employees?
Quais benefícios a empresa em que você trabalha oferece aos funcionários?

» Among other fringe benefits they offer a company car and health insurance.
Entre outros benefícios, eles oferecem um carro da empresa e plano de saúde.

» "The salary is not that good, but the perks are great", said Bill to a friend.
"O salário não é lá essas coisas, mas as mordomias são ótimas", disse Bill a um amigo.

Bens de uma empresa: veja "patrimônio" p. 92

Bônus; abono; bonificação: bonus

» Everyone in the sales department gets a bonus when the goals are reached.
Todos no departamento de vendas recebem um bônus quando as metas são alcançadas.

Brainstorming (técnica de dinâmica de grupo em que as pessoas apresentam suas idéias e sugestões a partir de um tema colocado): brainstorming

» Lots of new ideas came up when we had a brainstorming session.
Muitas idéias novas surgiram quando fizemos uma sessão de brainstorming.

C

Campanha publicitária: advertising campaign

» They are planning a big advertising campaign including e-mail marketing and billboards all over the city.
Eles estão planejando uma grande campanha publicitária incluindo marketing por e-mail e outdoors por toda a cidade.

Candidatar-se: to apply for/applied for/applied for

» "You have all the skills the position requires. Why don't you apply for it?", Tim asked Jane.
"Você tem todas as qualificações necessárias para a função. Por que não se candidata?", Tim perguntou a Jane.

Candidato(a) a emprego: applicant.   » Veja também "formulário de requisição de emprego" p. 81

» Have you interviewed all the applicants yet?
Você já entrevistou todos os candidatos?

Capaz de analisar e interpretar dados: able to analyze and interpret data

Capaz de concentrar-se e prestar atenção a detalhes: able to concentrate and pay attention to detail

Capaz de executar muitas tarefas ao mesmo tempo: multitasker

Capaz de motivar a equipe: able to motivate staff

Capaz de trabalhar sob pressão: able to work under pressure

Carga: cargo

» "Has the cargo been unloaded yet?", the factory manager asked Dave.
"A carga já foi descarregada?", o gerente da fábrica perguntou a Dave.

Carga de trabalho: workload

» "Our workload has practically doubled in the past few months. We need to hire more people soon", the factory manager explained to Mr. Rogers.
"Nossa carga de trabalho praticamente dobrou nos últimos meses. Precisamos contratar mais pessoas logo", o gerente da fábrica explicou ao sr. Rogers.

Cargo: position

» "The applicants we have interviewed so far are not qualified for the position", the human resources manager told Mr. Dawson.
"Os candidatos que entrevistamos até agora não são qualificados para o cargo", o gerente de recursos humanos disse ao sr. Dawson.

Cartão de visitas: business card

CEO (a pessoa com maior autoridade em uma empresa de grande porte): CEO (chief executive officer)

» The new CEO promised to make the company profitable again.
O novo CEO prometeu tornar a empresa lucrativa novamente.

Chefe de departamento: chief of the department; head of the department

» Jill doesn't seem to get along with the new chief of the department.
Jill não parece se dar bem com o novo chefe do departamento.

Cheio de energia: energetic

Cliente: customer

Código de barra: bar code

» The check out attendant ran the scanner over the bar code to check the price of the product.
O caixa passou o scanner no código de barras para conferir o preço do produto.

» Make sure to check the package to see if there is a bar code at the bottom.
Não deixe de olhar a embalagem para ver se há um código de barras na parte inferior.

Colega de trabalho: co-worker; colleague

» Mike has lunch with his co-workers at the company cafeteria every day.
Mike almoça com os colegas de trabalho no refeitório da empresa todos os dias.

Competência; perícia; habilidade específica; capacidade: expertise

» "Jason's expertise in IT would be ideal for our department", said Terry at the meeting.
"A competência em TI do Jason seria ideal para o nosso departamento", disse Terry na reunião.

Comportamento: behavior

» The company found the employee's behavior unacceptable and decided to fire him.
A empresa achou o comportamento do funcionário inaceitável e decidiu despedi-lo.

Comportar-se: to behave/behaved/behaved

» Employees are expected to behave according to the company's policy.
Os funcionários devem se comportar de acordo com a política da empresa.

Comprador: buyer. » Veja também "departamento de compras" p. 74

Compreensivo(a): understanding

» Mr. Harold was very understanding when we told him we had not reached the quarterly sales goal.
O sr. Harold foi bastante compreensivo quando lhe dissemos que não tínhamos alcançado a meta de vendas do trimestre.

Comprometido: committed

» Hard-working, committed employees are not easy to find these days.
Funcionários trabalhadores e comprometidos não são fáceis de encontrar hoje em dia.

Comprometimento; compromisso: commitment

» The company Jake works for has a commitment to quality.
A empresa para a qual Jake trabalha tem compromisso com a qualidade.

Computação: veja "tecnologia da informação" p. 99

Concorrência: competition

» The price of raw material has dropped due to the fierce competition among suppliers.
O preço da matéria-prima caiu devido à concorrência acirrada entre os fornecedores.

Confiável: reliable; dependable

» You can always count on Bill. He's a reliable employee.
Você pode sempre contar com o Bill. Ele é um funcionário confiável.

Concorrente; empresa concorrente: competitor

» What are your company's main competitors?
Quais são os principais concorrentes da sua empresa?

Congresso; convenção: congress; convention

» "Mr. Adams is in Mexico at a sales convention. Would you like to leave a message?", said Janet over the phone.
"O sr. Adams está no México em uma convenção de vendas. Gostaria de deixar recado?", disse Janet no telefone.

Consultor: consultant

Consultoria: consulting company

Contabilidade: accounting

Contador: accountant

Contratar; empregar: to hire/hired/hired; to employ/employed/employed

» Our company has just hired three new salesmen.
Nossa empresa acabou de contratar três novos vendedores.

» That big shoe factory employs over three hundred people.
Aquela grande fábrica de calçados emprega mais de trezentas pessoas.

Controle de qualidade: quality control

» Good quality control will help prevent financial losses.
Um bom controle de qualidade ajuda a evitar perdas financeiras.

Cooperar: to cooperate/cooperated/cooperated

» "Things would be a lot easier if all the employees cooperated", Mr. Harrison told Mike.
"As coisas seriam muito mais fáceis se todos os funcionários cooperassem", o sr. Harrison disse ao Mike.

Cooperação: cooperation

» "We'll need all the salesmen's cooperation if we are to reach the monthly goal", said the sales manager at the meeting.
"Vamos precisar da cooperação de todos os vendedores se quisermos alcançar a meta mensal", o gerente de vendas disse na reunião.

Corpo de funcionários; equipe; pessoal: staff

» "In order to be more productive you need to learn to delegate work to your staff", Mr. Davies told Richard.
"Para ser mais produtivo você precisa aprender a delegar trabalho para a sua equipe", o sr. Davies disse ao Richard.

Corretor de imóveis: real estate agent

Corretor de seguros: insurance agent

Cotação: quotation

» Jim asked the lawyer to give him a quotation for her monthly fees.
Jim pediu a advogada uma cotação de honorários mensal.

Criatividade: creativity

Criativo(a): creative

» "Harry is a very creative manager. I'm sure he'll come up with a solution to this problem", Mr. Newman told Frank.
Harry é um gerente muito criativo. Tenho certeza de que ele encontrará uma solução para esse problema", Mr. Newman told Frank.

Cuidadoso(a): careful

» Gary has always been very careful and methodical about everything he does.
Gary sempre foi muito cuidadoso e metódico com tudo o que faz.

Currículo; Curriculum Vitae; CV: résumé (EUA); CV (Ingl.)

» "The applicant's résumé wasn't good enough. That's why he wasn't hired", explained the human resources manager to a co-worker.
"O currículo do candidato não era bom o bastante. É por isso que ele não foi contratado", explicou o gerente de recursos humanos a um colega de trabalho.

CRM (gerenciamento de relacionamento com o cliente, sistema informatizado através do qual uma empresa busca desenvolver boas relações com seus clientes, mantendo informações sobre suas necessidades, etc.): CRM (customer relationship management)

» Having a strong CRM is the best way to keep existing customers.
Ter um bom sistema de CRM é a melhor forma de manter clientes atuais.

D

Dados: data

» "We need someone with good reasoning and who can interpret data properly", said Mr. Terrence to the human resources manager.
"Precisamos de alguém com bom raciocínio e que possa interpretar dados corretamente", disse o sr. Terrence para o gerente de recursos humanos.

Dar aviso prévio: to give notice

» In many Brazilian companies you must give a one-month notice before you leave the job.
Em muitas empresas brasileiras deve-se dar um mês de aviso prévio antes de deixar o emprego.

Dedicado(a): dedicated

» "Thanks to our dedicated staff we have been able to reach the monthly sales goals again", said Mr. Thompson.
"Graças a nossa equipe dedicada, fomos capazes de alcançar novamente a meta mensal de vendas ", disse o sr. Thompson.

Delegar: to delegate/delegated/delegated

» **"In order to be more productive you have to learn to delegate tasks to your staff", said Frank to a co-worker.**
"Para ser mais produtivo você precisa aprender a delegar tarefas para a sua equipe", disse Frank a um colega de trabalho.

Deletar; apagar: to delete/deleted/deleted

» **Make sure you delete all e-mail messages sent from unknown people since they might carry a virus.**
Não deixe de deletar todos os e-mails enviados por desconhecidos, pois podem ter vírus.

Demitir; despedir: to dismiss/dismissed/dismissed; to fire/fired/fired

» **Employees can now be dismissed for sexual harassment.**
Funcionários agora podem ser demitidos por assédio sexual.

» **"Did you know Tim was fired?", Bob asked his co-workers.**
"Vocês sabiam que o Tim foi demitido?", Bob perguntou aos colegas de trabalho.

Departamento administrativo: administrative department

Departamento de compras: purchasing department

» **Roger works as a buyer in the purchasing department of a big construction company.**
Roger trabalha como comprador no departamento de compras de uma grande construtora.

Departamento de contabilidade: accounting department

Departamento de expedição: shipping department

» **Who is in charge of the shipping department?**
Quem é responsável pelo departamento de expedição?

Departamento financeiro: financial department

Departamento de importação e exportação: import/export department

Departamento de marketing: marketing department

Departament de pesquisa e desenvolvimento: research and development department; R&D

Departamento de RH: human resources department; HR

Departamento de vendas: sales department

Departamento pessoal: personnel department

Despachar, transportar por navio, avião, caminhão, trem, etc.: to ship/shipped/shipped
» Veja também "departamento de expedição" p. 74

Desafio: challenge
» Barry is a proactive employee who enjoys responsibility and challenges.
Barry é um funcionário proativo que gosta de responsabilidade e desafios.

Designer; projetista: designer

Determinado(a): driven; determined
» Tim seems to be really driven to reach the monthly sales goals.
Tim parece estar mesmo determinado a alcançar as metas de vendas do mês.

Dever: duty/duties (pl.)
» "What were the daily duties of your previous job?", the interviewer asked the candidate.
"Quais eram seus deveres diários no seu emprego anterior?", o entrevistador perguntou
ao candidato.

Dia de folga: day off
» What do you usually do on your day off?
O que você geralmente faz no seu dia de folga?

Diferencial: competitive edge
» What's your company's main competitive edge in your opinion?
Na sua opinião, qual é o principal diferencial de sua empresa?

Diretor: director

Diretor administrativo: administrative director

Diretor comercial: commercial director

Diretor financeiro: financial director

Diretor industrial: industrial director

Diretor de marketing: marketing director

Diretor de recursos humanos: human resources director

Diretor de vendas: sales director

Diretoria: board of directors; board

» When is the board meeting scheduled?
Para quando está marcada a reunião da diretoria?

Disciplinado(a): disciplined

Discutir e apresentar idéias em grupo: to brainstorm/brainstormed/brainstormed » Veja
também "brainstorming" p. 68

» "Let's brainstorm this topic a little more. I'm sure we can come up with some more
ideas", said Bill at the meeting.
"Vamos discutir este tópico um pouco mais. Tenho certeza de que podemos ter mais
idéias", disse Bill na reunião.

Distribuir: to distribute/distributed/distributed

» Our company will distribute our product in the international market next year.
Nossa empresa vai distribuir nosso produto no mercado internacional no próximo
ano.

Distribuição: distribution

Divertido(a): fun

» James is a lot of fun. He makes everyone in the department laugh.
James é muito divertido. Ele faz todos no departamento rir.

Downsizing: veja "redução da força de trabalho; redução do número de funcionários de uma
empresa" p. 96

E

Economia: economics (ciência econômica); economy (economia de recursos ou de esforços,
parcimônia)

Economista: economist

Educado(a): polite

Empreendedor: entrepreneur

» One of the advantages of being an entrepreneur is that you are your own boss.
Uma das vantagens de ser um empreendedor é que você é seu próprio chefe.

Empregado(a), funcionário(a): employee

» Over one hundred employees work at that factory.
   Mais de cem funcionários trabalham naquela fábrica.

Empregador(a); empresa que emprega: employer

» That steel company is the biggest employer in the region.
   Aquela companhia de aço é a maior empregadora na região.

Empregar: to employ/employed/employed

» How many people does that big car plant employ?
   Quantas pessoas aquela grande montadora de automóveis emprega?

Emprego sem futuro: dead-end job

» Why don't you start looking for work with another company? You don't want to be
   stuck in a dead-end job forever, do you?
   Por que você não começa a procurar trabalho em alguma outra empresa? Você não quer
   ficar parado pelo resto da vida num emprego sem futuro, quer?

Empresa ponto-com: dot-com company

» There's a huge concentration of dot-com companies in Silicon Valley, California.
   Há uma grande concentração de empresas ponto-com no Vale do Silício, na Califórnia.

Empresário: businessman

Enérgico(a), ativo(a), vigoroso(a): energetic

Engenheiro(a): engineer

Engenheiro(a) civil: civil engineer

Engenheiro(a) de alimentos: food engineer

Engenheiro(a) de produção: production engineer

Engenheiro(a) de produto: product engineer

Engenheiro(a) elétrico: electrical engineer

Engenheiro(a) químico: chemical engineer

Engenheiro(a) mecânico: mechanical engineer

Engraçado(a): funny

Entrevista: interview
» The HR department is interviewing three candidates for the job.
O departamento de RH está entrevistando três candidatos para a vaga.

Entrevistado(a): interviewee

Entrevistador(a): interviewer

Entrevistar: to interview/interviewed/interviewed
» Not all applicants have been interviewed yet.
Nem todos os candidatos foram entrevistados ainda.

Entusiasmado(a): excited
» Barry is all excited about the new project.
Barry está todo entusiasmado com o novo projeto.

Enviar por e-mail; mandar um e-mail: to e-mail/e-mailed/e-mailed
» "I'll e-mail you the form later today", Frank told Clint over the phone.
"Vou lhe enviar o formulário por e-mail mais tarde", Frank disse para Clint pelo telefone.

Equilibrado(a): balanced
» Jason strikes me as a balanced and reliable employee.
Jason me parece um funcionário equilibrado e confiável.

Especialidade; habilidade específica: veja "competência" p. 70

Estagiário(a): intern
» Sam was an intern at an advertising agency when he was at university.
Sam foi estagiário em uma agência de publicidade quando estava na faculdade.

Estágio (profissional): internship
» Barry did an internship at a large software company when he was at college.
Barry fez estágio em uma grande empresa de software quando estava na faculdade.

Estande (em feiras comerciais, exposições): booth; stand

Estável: stable

Estressante: stressful

» **"We've had some very stressful situations at work recently", Neil told his wife.**
"Temos tido algumas situações muito estressantes no trabalho recentemente", Neil disse à esposa

Estresse: stress

» **"How do you handle stress?", the interviewer asked Jack.**
"Como você lida com o estresse?", o entrevistador perguntou a Jack..

Ética (subs): ethics

» **Professional ethics is unfortunately not always a rule in today's business world.**
Infelizmente a ética profissional nem sempre é uma regra no mundo corporativo atual.

Ético(a) (adj): ethical

» **You can rely on Heather. She's always been an ethical professional.**
Você pode confiar na Heather. Ela sempre foi uma profissional ética.

Exigente: demanding

Expansão econômica: veja "alta; aumento da atividade econômica" p. 64

Experiência de trabalho: work experience. » Veja também "experiente; com experiência" p. 79

» **It is important to build up good work experience before you look for another job.**
É importante desenvolver uma boa experiência de trabalho antes de procurar outro emprego.

Experiente; com experiência: experienced

» **We need to hire two more experienced salesmen.**
Precisamos contratar mais dois vendedores com experiência.

Extrovertido: outgoing; extroverted

F

Fábrica: plant; factory

» **Jake works for a car plant that employs over five hundred people.**
Jake trabalha para uma montadora de automóveis que emprega mais de quinhentas pessoas.

Fabricante: manufacturer

Fabricar: to manufacture/manufactured /manufactured

» **"What do they manufacture?", Brian asked a co-worker.**
"O que eles fabricam?", Brian perguntou a um colega de trabalho.

» **Apple manufactures computers.**
A Apple fabrica computadores.

Falir: to go bankrupt; to go bust (informal)

» **Many people lost their jobs when that shoe factory went bankrupt.**
Muitas pessoas perderam seus empregos quando aquela fábrica de calçados faliu.

Farmacêutico(a): pharmacist

Fazer bico: to moonlight/moonlighted/moonlighted

» **In order to earn some extra money, Bob moonlights as a waiter on weekends.**
Para ganhar um dinheiro extra, Bob faz bico de garçom nos finais de semana.

Fazer greve; entrar em greve: to go on strike

» **Traffic will be chaotic if the bus drivers decide to go on strike.**
O trânsito vai ficar caótico se os motoristas de ônibus decidirem fazer greve.

» **The car plant workers have gone on strike for a raise in their salaries.**
Os trabalhadores da montadora de automóveis entraram em greve por aumento de salário.

Fazer hora extra: to work overtime

» **"Some of the factory workers will have to work overtime if demand for our products keeps up", the factory manager told Mr. Williams.**
"Alguns dos funcionários da fábrica terão de fazer hora extra se a demanda pelos nossos produtos se mantiver em alta", o gerente da fábrica disse ao Sr. Williams.

Fazer um upgrade; atualizar um programa ou sistema de computação: to upgrade/ upgraded/upgraded

» **"I had to upgrade my hard drive to run that software", said Gary to a co-worker.**
"Tive de fazer um upgrade no meu disco rígido para rodar aquele software", disse Gary a um colega de trabalho.

Fechar uma empresa; encerrar as atividades: to close down a company

» **They will be forced to close down the company if business does not pick up.**
Eles serão forçados a encerrar as atividades se os negócios não melhorarem.

Feedback (conselho, crítica ou informação que é passada a uma empresa sobre um produto ou serviço, com o intuito de melhorá-lo): feedback

» **We'd appreciate if you could give us some feedback on the new product.**
Agradeceríamos se vocês pudessem nos dar um feedback sobre o novo produto.

80

Feira comercial: trade show; trade fair

» **Will your company have a booth at the trade show in Las Vegas this year?**
Sua empresa vai ter um estande na feira comercial em Las Vegas este ano?

Feriado: holiday

Férias: vacation (EUA); holiday (Ingl.). » Veja também "sair de férias" p. 97

» **"New employees are entitled to only a two-week vacation in their first year with the company", Mr. Clark told the applicant.**
"Novos funcionários têm direito a apenas duas semanas de férias no primeiro ano na empresa", o Sr. Clark disse ao candidato.

Filial: branch office. » Veja também "matriz, sede de empresa" p. 89

» **Our company has branch offices all over the country.**
Nossa empresa tem filiais por todo o país.

Fiscal: inspector

Físico(a): physicist

Fluxo de caixa: cash-flow

Formulário: form

Formulário de requisição de emprego: application form

» **"Can you please fill in this application form?", Mrs. Vaughan told the candidate.**
"Você pode por favor preencher este formulário de requisição de emprego?", a sra. Vaughan disse ao candidato.

Fornecedor: supplier

» **In order to get the best price the big supermarket chains usually play hardball with their suppliers.**
Para conseguir o melhor preço, as grandes cadeias de supermercado geralmente jogam duro com os fornecedores.

Fornecer: to supply/supplied/supplied

» **A Chinese company has been supplying us with raw material in the past few years.**
Uma empresa chinesa nos tem fornecido a matéria-prima nos últimos anos.

Franqueado: franchisee

Franqueador: franchiser

Franquia: franchise

Freelance; freelancer; frila (inf.) (profissional que trabalha por conta própria, sem vínculo empregatício): freelance
» Mary is a freelance photographer.
Mary é uma fotógrafa freelance.
» Bill used to have a full-time job with the New York Post, but now he works freelance from home.
Bill tinha um emprego em período integral no jornal New York Post, mas agora trabalha como freelance.

Frete: freight
» "Do you think it's possible to reduce the freight cost?", asked Brian at the meeting.
"Você acha possível reduzir o custo do frete?", perguntou Brian na reunião.

Frota: fleet
» Our company has a fleet of fifty-five trucks.
Nossa empresa tem uma frota de cinqüenta e cinco caminhões.
» Many moving companies have a fleet of trucks with their name and logo on them.
Muitas empresas de mudança têm uma frota de caminhões com seu nome e logotipo.

Fundador: founder
» Henry Ford was the founder of the Ford Motor Company.
Henry Ford foi o fundador da empresa Ford.

Fundar: to found/founded/founded
» Microsoft, the world's largest software company, was founded by Bill Gates and Paul Allen in 1975.
A Microsof, a maior empresa de software do mundo, foi fundada por Bill Gates e Paul Allen em 1975.

Funcionário; empregado: employee

Funcionário público: civil servant
» People who work for the government are called civil servants.
As pessoas que trabalham para o governo são chamadas de funcionários públicos.

Fundir-se; juntar-se comercialmente: to merge/merged/merged
» Profits went skyhigh after the two main companies in the pharmaceutical industry decided to merge.
Os lucros dispararam depois que as duas principais empresas na indústria farmacêutica decidiram fundir-se.

Fusão de empresas; fusão comercial: merger

» News of the merger between the two main competitors in the steel industry was released this morning.
Notícias da fusão entre as duas principais empresas concorrentes da indústria do aço foram reveladas esta manhã.

G

Gerência: management

Gerenciar: to manage/managed/managed

» "We need to find the right guy to manage this project", said Nick at the meeting.
"Precisamos encontrar o cara certo para gerenciar esse projeto", disse Nick na reunião.

Gerente: manager

Gerente administrativo: administrative manager

Gerente comercial: commercial manager

Gerente de marketing: marketing manager

Gerente de produção: production manager

Gerente de produto: product manager

Gerente de recursos humanos: human resources manager

Gerente de vendas: sales manager

Gerente financeiro: financial manager

Globalização: globalization

» Globalization has changed the world markets drastically.
A globalização mudou drasticamente os mercados mundiais.

Gratificante: gratifying; rewarding

Greve: strike. » Veja também "fazer greve; entrar em greve" p. 80

H

Habilidade: skill

Habilidade interpessoal: interpersonal skills

» **"Interpersonal skills are crucial for this position", said the human resources director.**
"Habilidade interpessoal é fundamental para essa função", disse o diretor de recursos humanos.

» **A managing position requires one to have interpersonal skills.**
Um cargo gerencial requer habilidade interpessoal.

Headhunter; caçador de talentos; profissional que recruta: headhunter

» **A headhunter was able to find Peter the exact job he wanted.**
Um headhunter conseguiu encontrar o emprego ideal para Peter.

» **The company was able to find a highly qualified employee for a managing position through a headhunter.**
A empresa conseguiu encontrar um funcionário altamente qualificado para um cargo gerencial através de um headhunter.

Hierarquia: hierarchy

História; reputação; experiência: track record

» **Our company is looking for someone with a proven track record in advertising.**
Nossa empresa está procurando alguém com experiência comprovada em propaganda.

» **Nokia has a great track record of producing high quality phones.**
A Nokia tem uma boa reputação como fabricante de telefones de alta qualidade.

Holding; empresa controladora: holding company

» **"As you can see in our organization chart there are three companies under the holding company", Jack explained at the meeting.**
"Como você pode ver em nosso organograma, há três empresas controladas pela holding", Jack explicou na reunião.

Honesto(a): honest

Hora extra: overtime. » Veja também "fazer hora extra" p. 80

Horário comercial: business hours

» **"Our normal business hours are from 8-6", explained the receptionist over the phone.**
"Nosso horário comercial normal é das 8h às 18h", explicou a recepcionista pelo telefone.

Horário de trabalho: working hours. » Veja também "turno de trabalho" p. 101

» What are your working hours?
Qual é o seu horário de trabalho?

» "Our working hours are 8 until 5", the clerk informed Mrs. Williams.
"Nosso horário de trabalho é das 8h até 17h", o atendente informou a sra. Williams.

Horário flexível de trabalho: flextime

» Someone working flextime has the flexibility to come to work at various times of the day.
Quem tem horário flexível de trabalho pode vir trabalhar em vários horários do dia.

» "With flextime, as long as I have done my eight hours, I can arrive and leave any time I want to", Brian told Josh.
"Com o horário flexível, contanto que eu faça as minhas oito horas, eu posso chegar e sair qualquer hora que eu quiser", Brian disse para Josh.

I

Implementação: implementation

Implementar: to implement/implemented/implemented

Indústria automobilística: automotive industry

» Japan has a strong automotive industry with the likes of Toyota and Honda.
O Japão tem uma indústria automobilística forte, com empresas como a Toyota e a Honda.

Informática: information technology; IT

» "We need to talk to the person in charge of the IT department", said Bill to a co-worker.
"Precisamos falar com a pessoa responsável pelo departamento de informática", disse Bill para um colega de trabalho.

Iniciativa: initiative

» "Initiative is a quality required for this position", said George to a co-worker.
"Iniciativa é uma qualidade exigida para esse cargo", disse George para um colega de trabalho.

Instalações comerciais: business facilities

» Our business facilities have a cafeteria, meeting rooms, offices and reception area.
Nossas instalações comerciais compreendem refeitório, salas de reunião, escritórios e recepção.

Intelectual: intellectual

Interação: interaction

Interagir: to interact/interacted/interacted
» Barry is an outgoing employee who interacts with all his co-workers.
Barry é um funcionário extrovertido que interage com todos os seus colegas de trabalho.

Intranet (rede privada e restrita que interliga os departamentos de uma empresa): intranet
» Many large companies have intranet interconnecting their departments.
A maioria das grandes empresas tem intranet interligando seus departamentos.
» All important messages are posted on the intranet of the company.
Todas as mensagens importantes são colocadas na intranet da empresa.

Inventário; estoque: inventory

Irrequieto(a): restless

J

Juros: interest. » Veja também "taxa de juros" p. 99

L

Lançamento: launch
» That big software company plans to do the launch of new products next quarter.
Aquela grande empresa de software planeja fazer o lançamento de novos produtos no próximo trimestre.

Lançar um produto: to launch a product
» That toy company has launched five new products in the past few months.
Aquela empresa de brinquedos lançou cinco novos produtos nos últimos meses.

Lazer: leisure
» What are your favorite leisure time activities?
Quais são as suas atividades de lazer favoritas?

Leal: loyal

LER (lesão por esforço repetitivo): RSI (repetitive strain injury)

» It's possible to get RSI from using a computer keyboard in the wrong way.
É possível contrair LER* ao usar o teclado do computador da forma errada.

Licença: leave of absence

» Our boss had to take a leave of absence because her father was ill.
Nossa chefe teve de sair de licença porque seu pai estava doente.

Licença-maternidade: maternity leave

» Sally is on maternity leave. She will only be back to work in four months' time.
Sally está de licença-maternidade. Ela só vai voltar ao trabalho daqui a quatro meses.

Licença médica: sick leave

» The factory manager will have to hire new people to fill in for some workers who are away on sick leave.
O gerente da fábrica terá de contratar novas pessoas para substituir alguns funcionários que estão de licença médica.

» "I had to take a sick leave because I caught a very bad flu", Will told a co-worker.
"Eu precisei sair de licença médica porque peguei uma gripe muito forte", Will disse a um colega de trabalho.

Líder: leader

Liderança: leadership

Liderar: to lead/led/led

Linguagem corporal: body language

Linha de produção: assembly line

» Assembly lines are most common with the production of cars.
As linhas de produção são mais usuais na fabricação de carros.

Locaute: lockout

» Just when the employees were planning to go on a strike over a dispute with the company, the board of directors decided on a lockout.
Justamente quando os funcionários estavam planejando entrar em greve por causa de um disputa com a empresa, os diretores decidiram fazer um locaute.

---

* LER não se trata de uma doença, e sim de um conjunto de síndromes relacionadas ao excesso de trabalho e à falta de boas condições ergonômicas de trabalho. Além disso, a terminologia LER tende a ser substituída por DORT (distúrbios osteomusculares relacionados ao trabalho).

Locomover-se (até o trabalho): to commute/commuted/commuted

» Many people don't commute to work anymore. They work from their homes.
Muitas pessoas não se locomovem mais até o trabalho. Elas trabalham em casa.

Logotipo: logo

» An advertising agency will think up a new logo for our company.
Uma agência de publicidade vai bolar um novo logotipo para a nossa empresa.

» The Nike logo is famous all over the world.
O logotipo da Nike é famoso no mundo inteiro.

Lucrativo; rentável: profitable

» The oil company decided to close down its subsidiary in Asia since it was not a profitable operation anymore.
A empresa de petróleo decidiu fechar a subsidiária na Ásia, pois a operação não era mais lucrativa.

Lucros e prejuízos: profits and losses. » Veja também "ponto de equilíbrio" p. 93

M

Manutenção: maintenance

» "Our machines stop once a month for maintenance", the factory manager explained to the visitors.
"Nossas máquinas param uma vez por mês para manutenção", explicou o gerente da fábrica aos visitantes.

Mão-de-obra: labor

» Many companies have their products manufactured in China and other Asian countries since labor is cheaper there.
Muitas empresas fabricam seus produtos na China e outros países asiáticos, pois a mão--de-obra lá é mais barata.

Mão-de-obra especializada: skilled labor

Mão-de-obra não especializada: unskilled labor

Marca registrada: trademark

Marcar uma reunião: arrange a meeting; set up a meeting

» "We need to arrange a meeting to discuss the advertising campaign for the new product", said Frank to his co-workers.

"Precisamos marcar uma reunião para discutir a campanha publicitária do novo produto", disse Frank aos colegas de trabalho.

Market share; participação de mercado: market share

» Thanks to the new sales strategy that company's market share has increased from 20% to 25%.
Graças à nova estratégia de vendas, a participação de mercado daquela empresa aumentou de 20% para 25%.

Matéria-prima: raw material

» Who are the main suppliers of raw material to your company?
Quais são os principais fornecedores de matéria-prima para sua empresa?

Matriz; sede de empresa: headquarters; head office. » Veja também "filial" p. 81

» The head office of our company is in Seattle.
A matriz de nossa empresa fica em Seattle.

Meio período; de meio expediente (adj.); em meio expediente (adv.): part-time. » Veja também "período integral, de período integral (adj.); em período integral (adv.)" p. 93

» Ted has a part-time job.
Ted trabalha meio período.

» Sheila works part-time as a waitress in a restaurant.
Sheila trabalha meio período como garçonete em um restaurante.

Mentor (pessoa com mais experiência em determinada área e que aconselha e ajuda outra pessoa menos experiente): mentor

» Having Gary as a mentor is sure great. He knows all about the food industry.
Ter Gary como mentor é realmente ótimo. Ele conhece tudo sobre a indústria alimentícia.

Metas de vendas: sales goals

» Do the salesmen in your company get a good bonus when they reach the sales goals?
Os vendedores em sua empresa recebem um bom bônus quando alcançam as metas de vendas?

Metódico(a): methodical

» "We need someone with a methodical profile for this position", said the human resources manager.
"Precisamos de alguém com um perfil metódico para este cargo", disse o gerente de recursos humanos.

Moeda corrente: currency

» The Australian dollar is the currency in Australia.
O dólar australiano é a moeda corrente na Austrália.

Mudar de emprego: to change jobs

» "I wish I could change jobs. I'm tired of filling out forms day in day out", said Clint to a co-worker.
"Gostaria de poder mudar de emprego. Estou cansado de preencher formulários todo os dias", disse Clint a um colega de trabalho.

N

Navegar na internet; visitar páginas da internet: to surf the web; to surf the internet

» Jim spends hours surfing the web every day.
Jim passa horas navegando na internet todos os dias.

Networking (prática de manter contato e encontrar-se com pessoas da mesma atividade profissional para troca de informações, apoio mútuo etc.): networking

» Attending conferences and seminars is a good way of doing networking.
Participar de conferências e seminários é uma boa forma de fazer networking.

» Networking is one of the most important things to do to find a job.
O networking é uma das coisas mais importantes de se fazer para encontrar um emprego.

Nicho de mercado: market niche

» "Maybe it's time to explore other market niches", said Greg at the meeting.
"Talvez seja o momento de explorar outros nichos de mercado", disse Greg na reunião.

Notável; excepcional; marcante: outstanding

» "The applicant we interviewed this morning has an outstanding résumé", said the human resources manager to her boss.
"O candidato que entrevistamos esta manhã tem um currículo excepcional", disse a gerente de recursos humanos para o chefe.

O

Orçamento: budget

» "We are having a meeting with the shareholders to review the yearly budget", said Bill to a co-worker.
"Vamos fazer uma reunião com os acionistas para rever o orçamento anual", disse Bill a um colega de trabalho.

Organização sem fins lucrativos: non-profit organization

» **Non-profit organizations use the money they earn to help people.**
As organizações sem fins lucrativos usam o dinheiro que ganham para ajudar as pessoas.

Organizado(a): organized

» **Martha is a very organized secretary.**
Martha é uma secretária muito organizada.

Organograma: organization chart

» **The organization chart of a company lays out exactly in what position each person is in each department.**
O organograma de uma empresa demonstra com clareza o cargo que cada pessoa ocupa em cada departamento.

Orientado por metas ou objetivos: goal-oriented

» **We need people who are goal-oriented to work in the sales department.**
Precisamos de pessoas com foco em metas para trabalhar no departamento de vendas.

ONG (organização não governamental): NGO (non-governmental organization)

» **Many NGOs help with social and environmental issues.**
Muitas ONGs contribuem para causas sociais e ambientais.

Operador de telemarketing: telemarketing operator; telemarketing attendant

Oportunidade de promoção: promotion opportunities

» **Does the company you work for offer promotion opportunities?**
A empresa para a qual você trabalha oferece oportunidades de promoção?

P

Paciente (adj): patient

» **Thanks for being so patient with me!**
Obrigado por ser tão paciente comigo!
» **You'll have to be patient and wait for your turn to be interviewed.**
Você vai ter que ser paciente e esperar a sua vez de ser entrevistado.

Paciente (subs): patient

» **"Does it hurt here?", doctor Harris asked the patient.**
"Dói aqui?", o doutor Harris perguntou ao paciente.

Participação de mercado: veja "market share" p. 89

Patrimônio financeiro de uma empresa: assets

Patrocinador: sponsor

Patrocinar: to sponsor/sponsored/sponsored

» **Lance Armstrong was sponsored by the US Postal Service for the Tour de France.**
Lance Armstrong foi patrocinado pela empresa de correios norte-americana durante a corrida Tour de France.

Patrocínio: sponsorship

Pausa; intervalo: break

» **"I think we all need a break. How about some coffee?", Mr. Harrison told his staff.**
"Acho que nós todos precisamos de uma pausa. Que tal um café?", o sr. Harrison disse a sua equipe.

Pauta: veja "agenda" p. 64

Pedido de demissão: resignation

» **Harry turned in his resignation after learning about the bad ethics of the company.**
Harry entregou seu pedido de demissão depois que soube que a empresa não era ética.

Pedir concordata: to file for chapter eleven

» **Companies in financial difficulties sometimes have no other choice but to file for chapter 11 and try to bounce back.**
Empresas em dificuldades econômicas às vezes não têm escolha a não ser pedir concordata e tentar recuperar-se.

Pedir demissão: to resign/resigned/resigned

» **Everyone was taken by surprise when Mark decided to resign, after being with the company for over ten years.**
Fomos todos pegos de surpresa quando Mark decidiu pedir demissão após mais de dez anos na empresa.

Perfeccionista: perfectionist

» **All the employees in our department find it hard to put up with the new manager's perfectionist style.**
Todos os funcionários em nosso departamento acham difícil agüentar o estilo perfeccionista do novo gerente.

Perfil: profile

» What kind of profile is needed for this position?
Que tipo de perfil é necessário para esse cargo?

Período integral; de período integral (adj.); em período integral (adv.): full-time. »
Veja também "meio período, de meio expediente (adj.); em meio expediente (adv.)" p. 89

» Rose is a very active woman. She has two kids, works full-time, and still finds time to work out at the gym.
Rose é uma mulher bastante ativa. Ela trabalha em período integral, tem dois filhos e ainda encontra tempo para malhar na academia.

» Jake has never really had a full-time job.
Jake nunca realmente teve um emprego em período integral.

Pesquisa e desenvolvimento: research and development; R&D

Planilha eletrônica: spreadsheet. » Veja também "processador de texto" p. 94

» Jerry can use spreadsheets, word processors and all the major software very well.
Jerry sabe usar muito bem planilhas eletrônicas, processadores de texto e todos os principais programas.

Plano de carreira: career plan

» Does the company you work for offer a career plan?
A empresa para a qual você trabalha oferece plano de carreira?

Plano de pensão: pension plan

» Among other fringe benefits, the company offers their employees a private pension plan.
Entre outros benefícios, a empresa oferece a seus funcionários um plano privado de pensão.

Plano de saúde: health plan

» Does the company you work for offer a health plan to all its employees?
A empresa em que você trabalha oferece plano de saúde para todos os funcionários?

Política; norma de conduta: policy

» What's your company's policy regarding smoking?
Qual é a política de sua empresa no que diz respeito a fumar?

Ponto de equilíbrio: breakeven point. » Veja também "atingir o ponto de equilíbrio" p. 66

» They have been very successful with their new business. They've reached breakeven point in just a couple of months!
Eles tiveram muito sucesso com o novo negócio. Atingiram o ponto de equilíbrio em apenas alguns meses!

Pontos fortes e pontos fracos: strengths and weaknesses

» What are your company's strengths and weaknesses compared to its competition?
Quais são os pontos fortes e os pontos fracos da sua empresa, se comparada à concorrência?

Pragmático(a): pragmatic

Prazo; data-limite: deadline

» "The deadline for enrolling in the fiscal seminar is August, 3rd", said Nick to his co-workers.
"A data-limite para matrícula no seminário fiscal é 3 de agosto", disse Nick aos colegas de trabalho.

Previdência social: social security; welfare

Prioridade: priority (pl. priorities)

Priorizar: to prioritize/prioritized/prioritized

Proativo(a): proactive

» This position requires someone with a proactive profile.
Este cargo requer alguém com um perfil proativo.

Processador de texto: word processor.   » Veja também "planilha eletrônica" p. 93

PIB (Produto Interno Bruto): GDP (Gross Domestic Product)

PNB (Produto Nacional Bruto): GNP (Gross National Product)

Professor(a): teacher

Professor universitário: professor

Projetista; designer: designer

Programa de treinamento e desenvolvimento: training and development program

» The Human Resource Department is in charge of administering the company's training and development programs.
O departamento de recursos humanos é responsável pela organização dos programas de treinamento e desenvolvimento da empresa.

Promotor de vendas: sales representative; sales rep.

Psicanalista: psychoanalyst

Psicólogo (a): psychologist

Público-alvo: target audience
» That toy company's target audience is children aged between 5 and 12.
O público-alvo daquela empresa de brinquedos é de crianças entre 5 e 12 anos de idade.

Q

Quadro de avisos: noticeboard

Qualificações: qualifications

Qualificado(a): qualified
» "I'm not sure the candidate we interviewed this morning is qualified for this position",
said the human resources manager.
"Não tenho certeza se o candidato que entrevistamos hoje de manhã é qualificado para
esse cargo", disse o gerente de recursos humanos.

Químico: chemist

R

Recepcionista: receptionist

Recolocação de executivos: outplacement

Recuperar(-se): to bounce back
» It took nearly a year for the company to bounce back from its financial crisis.
Levou quase um ano para a empresa se recuperar da crise financeira.

Recrutamento: recruitment
» One of the job duties of HR is recruitment of new workers.
Uma das funções do RH é recrutar novos funcionários.

Recrutar: to recruit/recruited/recruited
» The company is recruiting three new employees for the sales department.
A empresa está recrutando três novos funcionários para o departamento de vendas.

Recursos Humanos (RH): human resources (HR)

» Mrs. Williams is in charge of the HR department in our company.
O sr. Williams é responsável pelo departamento de RH em nossa empresa.

Redução do número de funcionários de uma empresa: downsizing

Reduzir o número de pessoas que trabalham em uma empresa a fim de cortar custos:
to downsize/downsized/downsized

» Many companies are sometimes forced to downsize their workforce to cope with financial difficulties.
Muitas empresas são às vezes forçadas a reduzir o número de funcionários para lidar com dificuldades financeiras.

Reengenharia: reengineering

Refeitório de empresa: cafeteria

» Nick often has lunch at the company cafeteria.
O Nick freqüentemente almoça no refeitório da empresa.

Referencial de excelência: veja "benchmark" p. 68

Relação custo-benefício: cost-benefit ratio

» We'd better compare the cost-benefit ratio of the two propositions in order to make the right choice.
É melhor compararmos a relação custo-benefício das duas propostas a fim de fazermos a escolha correta.

Relacionamento; rapport; afinidade; entrosamento: rapport

» Peter has an excellent rapport with all his co-workers.
Peter tem um relacionamento excelente com todos os seus colegas de trabalho.

Relações públicas (RP): public relations (PR)

Relatório: report

Responsável: responsible

Reportar-se a: to report to

» As marketing manager, Leo reports to Mr. Davis, the marketing director.
Como gerente de marketing, Leo se reporta ao Sr. Davis, o diretor de marketing.

Representante: representative; rep

Rotatividade de funcionários: turnover

» The salary they pay at that company is really low. It's no wonder they have such a high turnover.
O salário que eles pagam naquela empresa é realmente baixo. Não é de se admirar que eles tenham uma alta rotatividade de funcionários.

» The high turnover among factory workers is a problem the company hasn't been able to solve yet.
A alta rotatividade de funcionários da fábrica é um problema que a empresa ainda não conseguiu resolver.

S

Sair de férias: to go on vacation (EUA); to go on holiday (Ingl.)

» "I'm going on vacation next month", said Greg to a co-worker.
"Vou sair de férias no mês que vem", disse Greg para um colega de trabalho.

Salário: salary (pago mensalmente); wage(s) (pago por hora, dia ou semana)

Salário mínimo: minimum wage

» The minimum wage in the USA is around seven dollars an hour.
O salário mínimo nos Estados Unidos é aproximadamente sete dólares por hora.

Secretário(a): secretary

Seguro-saúde: health insurance

Sensato(a): sensible

Sensível: sensitive

Sério(a): serious

Ser responsável por: to be in charge of

» "May I talk to the person in charge of the purchasing department, please?", Dave asked the operator.
"Posso falar com a pessoa responsável pelo departamento de compras, por favor?", David pediu à telefonista

Sincero(a): sincere

Sindicato: union; labor union

» The union and company representatives came to an agreement after two hours of negotiation.
Os representantes do sindicato e da empresa chegaram a um acordo após duas horas de negociação.

Site de busca: search engine

» Google is one of the most popular search engines.
O Google é um dos sites de busca mais conhecidos.

Sociável: sociable; gregarious

Sociedade (comercial): partnership

Sócio: partner

Solidário(a): sympathetic

Subsidiária: subsidiary

» A subsidiary is a smaller company controlled by a larger company.
Uma subsidiária é uma companhia menor controlada por uma maior.

Substituir alguém: to fill in for someone

» "We need to hire someone to fill in for Emma while she is away on maternity leave", said Ron at the meeting.
"Precisamos contratar alguém para substituir Emma enquanto ela estiver de licença--maternidade", disse Ron na reunião.

» As one of the factory workers was sick, the manager asked Bill if he could fill in.
Como um dos funcionários da fábrica estava doente, o gerente perguntou a Bill se ele podia substitui-lo.

Supervisionar: to supervise/supervised/supervised

» "As a manager I supervised a staff of 33 people", said Mark at the interview.
"Como gerente eu supervisionei uma equipe de 33 pessoas", disse Mark na entrevista.

Supervisor: supervisor

T

Tarefa: task

» "What types of tasks can be delegated in your opinion?", the interviewer asked the candidate.
"Que tipos de tarefas podem ser delegadas, na sua opinião?", o entrevistador perguntou ao candidato.

Taxa de câmbio: exchange rate

» What's the exchange rate of the dollar to the real now?
Qual é a taxa de câmbio do dólar para o real agora?

Taxa de juros: interest rate

Técnico: technician

Tecnologia da informação (TI): information technology (IT)

» Most of the best American IT companies today are in Silicon Valley, close to the San Francisco Bay area.
A maioria das melhores empresas de tecnologia da informação norte-americanas está localizada no Vale do Silício, próximo da baía de San Francisco.

Tecnologia de ponta: state-of-the-art technology; cutting-edge technology

» State-of-the-art technology in computers is available to anyone who can afford it these days.
Hoje em dia, a tecnologia de ponta em computadores está disponível para qualquer um que possa pagar.

Telefonista: operator

Tendência: trend

» Attending lectures and conferences is a good way to keep updated on the latest market trends.
Participar de palestras e congressos é uma boa forma de se manter atualizado em relação às tendências de mercado mais recentes.

» Mp3 players are a big trend in the gadget market.
Os MP3 players são uma forte tendência no mercado de aparelhos eletrônicos.

Terceirização: outsourcing

» Outsourcing of non-core activities is a usual practice among many companies nowadays.
Atualmente, a terceirização das atividades não-principais é prática comum em muitas empresas.

Terceirizar: to outsource/outsourced/outsourced

» The IT department of our company has been outsourced.
O departamento de informática de nossa empresa foi terceirizado.

» Many US companies are outsourcing their call centers to India.
Muitas empresas norte-americanas estão terceirizando suas centrais de atendimento telefônico para a Índia.

Ter um bom relacionamento com; dar-se bem com: to get along with

» Peter doesn't get along with his boss. As a matter of fact he is thinking of changing jobs.
Peter não se dá bem com o chefe. De fato, ele está pensando em mudar de emprego.

Teste de aptidão: aptitude test

Tirar dia(s) de folga: to take time off

» "I was wondering if I could take next Friday off. I really need to take care of some family matters", Diane told her boss.
"Eu estava pensando se poderia tirar a próxima sexta-feira de folga. Eu preciso muito cuidar de alguns assuntos familiares", Diane disse ao chefe.

Tocar uma empresa; gerenciar; ser o responsável: to run a company

» Who's running the company since Mr. Smith retired?
Quem está tocando a empresa desde que o sr. Smith se aposentou?

Trabalhar bastante; dar duro: to work hard

» Jim has always worked very hard. It's no wonder he became a director in such a short time.
Jim sempre trabalhou muito. Não é de admirar que ele tenha se tornado diretor em tão pouco tempo.

Trabalho de equipe: teamwork

» "In order to achieve our goals, teamwork is essential", said the sales director at the meeting.
"Para que possamos atingir nossas metas, o trabalho de equipe é essencial", disse o diretor de vendas na reunião.

Trabalho sazonal: seasonal work

» Mark plans to do some seasonal work in the summer to save money for a car.
Mark planeja fazer trabalho sazonal no verão para economizar dinheiro e comprar um carro.

Trabalho voluntário: volunteer work
» Nick does volunteer work distributing soup to the homeless.
Nick faz trabalho voluntário distribuindo sopa aos sem-teto.

Traços de personalidade: personality traits
» "We do not only take into account the candidates' work experience but their personality traits as well", said the human resources analyst to a co-worker.
"Não levamos em conta apenas a experiência de trabalho dos candidatos, mas os traços de personalidade também", disse o analista de recursos humanos para um colega de trabalho.

Tradutor(a): translator

Turno de trabalho: shift
» "If demand for our products keeps up we'll have to start thinking of a third shift", said the factory manager at the meeting.
"Se a demanda pelos nossos produtos se mantiver em alta, nós teremos de começar a pensar em um terceiro turno de trabalho", disse o gerente da fábrica na reunião.
» Mike works on the night shift.
Mike trabalha no turno da noite.

U

Unir-(se); fundir-(se): to merge/merged/merged. » Veja também "fusão de empresas" p. 83
 The two main competitors in the software industry have decided to merge.
Os dois principais concorrentes da indústria de software decidiram fundir-se.

Usina elétrica: power plant

V

Vaga; emprego disponível: opening
» Does the company you work for have any openings right now?
A empresa para a qual você trabalha tem empregos disponíveis no momento?

Valor agregado: added value

Varejo: retail. » Veja também "atacado" p. 66

Vendedor (em uma empresa): salesman

Vendedor (em uma loja): clerk; salesclerk; salesperson

Veterinário(a): veterinarian; vet

W

Web designer (profissional que projeta e desenvolve sites): webdesigner
» Our webdesigner is working on creating a new website for our business.
  Nosso web designer está trabalhando na criação de um novo site para o nosso negócio.

Webmaster (responsável por um site na internet): webmaster

Workaholic (pessoa que é viciada em trabalho; que só pensa em trabalhar): workaholic
» "Do you consider yourself a workaholic?", the interviewer asked the applicant.
  "Você se considera um workaholic?", o entrevistador perguntou ao candidato.

7. KEY TO PRACTICE SETS
Respostas aos exercícios práticos

PRACTICE SET 1

A
1. "What types of **tasks** can be delegated in your opinion?", the interviewer asked the candidate.
2. "Could you please e-mail your **résumé** to us?", the human resources analyst told Claire over the phone.
3. This position requires someone with a **proactive** profile.
4. "Make sure you bring some business cards. We'll certainly do some **networking** at the conference tomorrow", said Bill to a co-worker.
5. "In order to achieve our goals, **teamwork** is essential", said the sales director at the meeting.
6. Many companies try to **recruit** at job fairs.
7. Doing **volunteer work** such as looking after elderly people or helping orphaned children can help enhance your life.
8. "We need to hire someone to fill in for Liz while she is away on **maternity leave**", said Brian at the meeting.
9. How many people does that factory **employ**?
10. "We won't be able to reach the goals without everyone's **commitment**", explained Mr. Clark at the meeting.

B
1. c
2. c
3. a
4. b
5. b

C
1. i
2. d
3. h
4. f
5. g
6. b
7. j
8. c
9. a
10. e

PRACTICE SET 2

A
1. The shareholders held a meeting to discuss the **profits** for the last quarter.
2. "I think we all need a **break**. Come on, let's have some coffee", said the manager to his staff.
3. The HR department is **interviewing** three candidates for the job.
4. "Are you looking for a part-time job or a **full-time** job?", the interviewer asked Joan at the interview.

5. The company Brian works for has a very high **turnover** of staff.
6. We were all surprised to hear David **resigned** after being with the company for more than fifteen years.
7. Nick works on the night **shift**.
8. "As a manager I **supervised** a staff of 15 people", said Greg at the interview.
9. "We'll have to **hire** more people and accquire new machines if demand for our products keeps up", the factory manager told Mike.
10. One of the job duties of HR is **recruitment** of new workers.

B

1. c
2. a
3. b
4. c
5. b

C

1. h
2. j
3. f
4. i
5. g
6. c
7. e
8. a
9. d
10. b

PRACTICE SET 3

A

1. We always come up with lots of new ideas when we have a **brainstorming** session.
2. "If demand for our products keeps up we'll have to start thinking of a third **shift**", said the factory manager at the meeting.
3. It's always important to carry your business card in case you decide to **network**.
4. "Let's schedule a meeting to talk about the **advertising campaign** for the new product", Mr. Wilcox told Eliot.
5. "Why don't you take a look at the **classified ads**? You might find a good job opportunity", said Susan to a friend.
6. Gary is a friendly guy and has a very good **rapport** with all his co-workers.
7. Kim doesn't work all day long. She has a **part-time** job.
8. "Did you have to work **overtime** at your previous job?", the interviewer asked the candidate.
9. **Outsourcing** of non-core activities is a usual practice among many companies nowadays.
10. Many American college students do **seasonal work** in the summer to save money for their classes.

B

1. c
2. c
3. d
4. c
5. b

C

1. c
2. h
3. a
4. g
5. i
6. j
7. d
8. b
9. e
10. f

PRACTICE SET 4

A

1. The company Roger works for employs a total of 57 **staff**.
2. Bill used to have a full-time job in the pharmaceutical industry, but now he works as a **freelance** consultant.
3. "One of my **duties** at my previous job was to supervise the store clerks", said the applicant to the interviewer.
4. "They offer a company car and health insurance among other **fringe benefits**", said Ralph to a friend.
5. Certain types of tasks cannot be **delegated**.
6. "What are your **strengths** and weaknesses in your opinion?", the interviewer asked Brian at the interview.
7. Doing an **internship** is the best way of gaining practical job experience.
8. Tom is a **proactive** employee who enjoys responsibility and challenges.
9. "I like to go to the park and get a suntan on my **day off**", Jack told a co-worker.
10. Learning a second language can give you a **competitive edge** when looking for a job.

B

1. c
2. a
3. b
4. d
5. d

C

1. g
2. j
3. h
4. i
5. f
6. e
7. b
8. c
9. d
10. a

PRACTICE SET 5

A

1. "Why don't you check out an **employment agency**? They might have just the job for you", Ruth advised a friend.
2. That big company's procedures are a **benchmark** for its competitors.
3. "Being an **entrepreneur** is exciting because you are your own boss, but it is also quite time consuming", explained Roger to a friend.
4. Many companies buy wholesale and then sell in their store at a **retail** price.
5. The **noticeboard** lists announcements regarding job openings and events in the company.
6. Frank plans to move to Florida when he **retires**.
7. "We have to find out why we've had so much **absenteeism** in the last two months", Bill told the factory manager.
8. Over two hundred **employees** work at that big car plant.

9. Many companies prefer to concentrate on their **core business** and outsource other departments.

10. "We need to see a **sample** of the product before buying", said the purchasing manager at the meeting.

B

1. b
2. c
3. a
4. b
5. d

C

1. e
2. d
3. f
4. b
5. a
6. c
7. j
8. i
9. h
10. g

8. AUDIO GUIDE - TRACK AND PAGE
Guia do Áudio - Faixa e página

Track 1: Job interview 1 - Career in sales p. 9
Track 2: Job interview 2 - Career in finance p. 11
Track 3: Job interview 3 - Management interview p. 12
Track 4: Job interview 4 - Changing job fields p. 14
Track 5: Job interview 5 - General job interview p. 15
Track 6: Job interview 6 - Behavioral job interview p. 16
Track 7: Job interview 7 - Career in teaching p. 18
Track 8: Job interview 8 - Informational job interview p. 19
Track 9: Job interview 9 - Secretary job interview p. 20
Track 10: Job interview 10 - Career in manufacturing p. 21
Track 11: Job interview 11 - An inappropriate interview p. 23
Track 12: Job interview 12 - Career in information technology p. 24
Track 13: Job interview questions 1 p. 27
Track 14: Job interview questions 2 p. 27
Track 15: Job interview questions 3 p. 28
Track 16: Job interview questions 4 p. 29
Track 17: Job interview questions 5 p. 29
Track 18: Job interview questions 6 p. 29
Track 19: Job interview questions 7 p. 30
Track 20: Job interview questions 8 p. 30
Track 21: Job interview questions 9 p. 31
Track 22: Job interview questions 10 p. 31
Track 23: Job interview questions 11 p. 32
Track 24: Job interview questions 12 p. 32
Track 25: Job interview questions 13 p. 32
Track 26: Job interview questions 14 p. 33
Track 27: Job interview questions 15 p. 33
Track 28: Interviewee's questions 1-27 p. 47-49

SOBRE OS AUTORES

JOSÉ ROBERTO A. IGREJA

Professor de inglês e responsável pelo site bilíngue www.dialectoenglish.com.br, atua no segmento de cursos de língua inglesa **in-company** há mais de quinze anos. Graduado em Língua e Literatura Inglesa pela PUC (SP), residiu em Londres, onde fez cursos de especialização. Possui os certificados de proficiência em inglês das universidades americanas BYU-Brigham Young University (Salt Lake City, Utah) e Michigan.

É autor dos livros **Fale tudo em Inglês!**, **How do you say... in English? – Expressões coloquiais e perguntas inusitadas para quem estuda ou ensina Inglês!**, sucesso entre os professores e estudantes de inglês, **Falsos Cognatos – Looks can be deceiving!**, **False Friends**, e coautor, com **Jonathan T. Hogan**, dos livros **Phrasal Verbs** e **Essential Phrasal Verbs**. É também coautor, com Joe Bailey Noble III, dos livros **American Idioms!** e **Essential American Idioms**, publicados pela Disal Editora.

ROBERT C. YOUNG

Natural do Tennessee (EUA.), é professor de inglês há oito anos, tendo residido e ensinado inglês em San Francisco (California), Japão e atualmente no Brasil. Especialista em inglês comercial, é graduado em Comunicações pela Universidade do Tennessee em Chattanooga e possui certificado de professor de inglês como língua estrangeira. Antes de se dedicar integralmente ao ensino trabalhou como gerente de relação e atendimento ao cliente durante cinco anos.

CONHEÇA TAMBÉM:

Acesse: www.disaleditora.com.br

COMO ACESSAR O ÁUDIO

Todo o conteúdo em áudio referente a este livro, você poderá encontrar em qualquer uma das seguintes plataformas:

Ao acessar qualquer uma dessas plataformas, será necessário a criação de uma conta de acesso (poderá ser a versão gratuita). Após, pesquise pelo título completo do livro, ou pelo autor ou ainda por **Disal Editora**, localize o álbum ou a playlist e você terá todas as faixas de áudio mencionadas no livro.

Para qualquer dúvida, entre em contato com **marketing@disaleditora.com.br**

IMPORTANTE:
Caso você venha a encontrar ao longo do livro citações ou referências a CDs, entenda como o áudio acima indicado.

Este livro foi composto na fonte Interstate e impresso setembro de 2021
pela Forma Certa, sobre papel offset 75g/m².